The Newest

WEBER

GRILL COOKBOOK

THE ULTIMATE GUIDE TO MASTER YOUR WEBER GRILL WITH FLAVORFUL RECIPES AND STEP-BY-STEP TECHNIQUES FOR SMART PEOPLE

ANGELICA MILLER

CONTENTS

BAKING RECIPES 52

INTRODUCTION

How Your Weber Wood Pellet Grill Works

The name itself refers to the method of heating. Pellet grills use a different fuel to traditional grills (which rely upon sources like charcoal or gas)–they use up and burn wooden pellets. These wooden pellets look like little tablets or tiny rolled cigars; they're actually just compressed sawdust.

These wooden pellets are rotated into the fire pot, where they are exposed to intense heat, combust and emit heat and smoke of their own. This process is stoked by an internal fan, which then sends and distributes the heat throughout the grill. As you can see, this is a different method of heating–almost a combination of traditional ovens and flame cooking.

The method of cooking is called convection heating, which is the same method used by traditional smoke boxes.

The advantage of this is that the food is separated from the fire by a metal plate–which means there are no flare-ups and no grease falls into the fire pit (which can, in turn, burn up and produce an unwelcome flavor, along with being a pain to clean).

Seeing the Benefits of Your Weber Wood Pellet Grill

1.   Easy To Manage Temperature

One of biggest obstacles people have when it comes to grilling and smoking meats is getting the fire started and controlling the temperatures.

If folks want to use a charcoal grill then they deal with getting the charcoal lit, adjusting the vents, waiting for temperatures to stabilize, adding more fuel during a cook, etc. If they are using a gas grill then getting it lit is easy but dialing in a temperature is difficult. Gas grills are designed for Low, Medium and High. What exactly those settings means is going to depend upon your grill, the ambient weather, etc.

Dealing with temperature control is the problem that dives so many people to using electric smokers where they can just dial in a temperature, sit back and relax.

When it comes to temperature control, using a pellet smoker is just as easy as using an electric smoker! You dial in a temperature, wait 15-20 minutes for the grill to stabilize and then start grilling!

2.   Flavor Is An Upgrade Over Electric And Propane

Without question, meat cooked on a pellet grill tastes better than meat cooked with an electric smoker or on a gas grill.

When you use an electric smoker the smoke flavor comes from smoldering wood chips that have to be replenished throughout the cook. When you are cooking on a pellet grill the smoke comes from the continually burning wood. The smoke from burning wood smells and tastes better than that from smoldering wood and gives a better smoke ring to boot. Same goes for meat cooked on a gas grill or smoker.

3.   Minimal Flare Ups

The basic design of almost all pellet grills places shields between the flames in the fire pot and the dripping grease. This design has the intrinsic benefit of reducing flare ups to just about zero.

If you have been grilling on a cheap gas grill or directly over lit charcoal then you know that if you are not paying attention then a sudden flare up can happen and scorch whatever you are cooking.

4.   Relatively Large Capacity

It doesn't cost much more money for a manufacturer to produce a large pellet grill vs a small one. The core expenses of the stand, electronics, auger, fan, smoke stack, pellet hopper, etc are constant. The only difference is making the cook chamber a little longer and the grates a little bigger.

Better to Use Your Wood Pellet Grill

1.   Use Your Pellet Grill Like You Use Your Oven

One of the simplest and best tricks I have learned is to use your pellet grill like you use your oven. Not every food is great with smoke added, but most things are! So experiment.

Any recipe that calls for roasting or baking in your kitchen oven can be transferred to your pellet smoker, simply by cooking for the same length of time and at the same temperature.

2.   Use a Thermometer, Not Your Clock

Following on from the above oven tip, using a thermometer to gauge the internal temperatures of your meat will ensure a better cook rather than using time alone.

After all, it might have been cooking for the suggested time, but if it doesn't reach the right temperature inside, you could severely overcook your food. Or worse, undercook it and make yourself and your guests very ill.

Using a thermometer will also save you from opening the cooking chamber, just to keep checking on the progress of your meat.

The saying goes 'if you're looking, you ain't cooking!'. This is because as you open the door, you let all the heat escape, preventing all that hot smokey goodness from progressing the cook.

So, if your pellet smoker doesn't come with an integrated thermometer, we recommend investing in a good quality, 3rd party digital one. This way, you can monitor the cook via your thermometer and let the grill do its thing!

3.   Use Those Upper Racks

Not only do upper racks give you extra space inside your grill, but they also mean the meat you've placed on them is further from the heat source.

This means the meat is being cooked more by convection, rather than radiant heat, which offers a more even cook.

Utilize every space and rack you have, and you'll also get more bang for your buck with the wood pellets you burn, as well as have a lot more food to go around!

4.   Get Your Reverse Searing On

To sear or reverse sear? That is the question! But know that pellet grills are brilliant at reverse searing your meat, and not enough grillers do it!

To get that medium-rare finish edge to edge, with a perfectly seared smokey edge, we recommend you learn how to reverse sear.

Think of this process, almost like sous vide cooking. You create the perfect finish throughout the entire steak that you are looking for, cooking with a very low and gentle heat, to ensure none of it, not even the surface, is overcooked.

Only after reaching the perfect doneness throughout, do you then sear to create the Maillard crust and caramelized edge that creates a succulent sensory experience on top of that tender meat.

Depending on the model of your pellet grill and what you're cooking, set your grill temperature to 225f and place your meat in.

Once the internal temperature of your meat reaches 125f, which typically takes 45 minutes to an hour for a 2" thick steak (for medium-rare), take your meat out.

Crank up the grill to 500f, allowing it to heat through thoroughly, and then move the meat back into the grill, on a lower rack, and sear it for a couple of minutes with the lid closed, turning it once, until you have a great crust.

The result will be perfectly medium-rare meat throughout, with a great crust. And not a hint of that grey, overcooked outer edge you often get with the traditional sear.

5.   Creating a Smokier Flavor

This tip is for those larger cuts of meat that you want to pull more smoke into, such as beef brisket or a chuck roast.

Smoke loves cold meats, 'condensing' onto the surface more readily than it does to warm surfaces. So the colder it is, the more chance you'll give the smoke to adhere to it.

So, instead of allowing your meat to come up to room temperature – as many recipes request you to do – whip it straight out of the fridge with the dry rub you placed on it the night before and put it straight into the pellet smoker.

As usual, set it to a low smoking temperature and allow it that extra time with the smoke, to get a more pronounced smoke flavor.

Cleaning Tricks for Your Weber Wood Pellet Grill

1.Burning Off the Grill after Grilling

Depends on how much gunk/food residue is left, I like to give the grill a good brush down, then fire up to max temperature for 5 minutes. Then a follow up brushing and turning off/cooling down sequence.

2. Grill Cleaning a Few Options

You can just go for a wire brush (check that you pellet grill grill can handle an abrasive brush, some can, some can't) or get a specific tool that is a bit more thorough, design specific.

TIP: If you don't have either of these tools, you can use a scrunched up bit of tin foil to clean in between the grates.

If your not into cleaning the pellet grill after each cook, a minimum of cleaning after each 40 lb of pellets should be done.

3.Ash Removal After Each Cook

Once off and cool I take the ash out, do a quick check inside to see if there is any grease build up.

Even though there won't be much, I like to always empty the ash after a cook.

Getting rid of the ash is always a good idea after each cook, and some pellet grills like the Campchef's have simple pull out knobs for ash removal.

4. Clean Probe In Pellet Grill

The internal temperature probe, once cooled, should have a wipe.

A small amount of vinegar and water, with a scourer or scrubber, is an easy technique to keep the probe clean.

SEAFOOD RECIPES

Whole Vermillion Red Snapper

Servings: 6
Cooking Time: 20 Minutes

Ingredients:

- 1 Whole Vermillion Red Snapper, scaled & gutted
- 4 Clove garlic, chopped
- 1 Whole lemon, thinly sliced
- 2 Sprig rosemary sprigs
- sea salt and freshly ground black pepper

Directions:

1. Supply your smoker with wood pellets and follow the start-up procedure. Preheat the grill, with the lid closed, to High heat.
2. Stuff the cavity of the fish with chopped garlic. Sprinkle the fish with sea salt, pepper, rosemary, and lemon.
3. Grill fish directly on the grill grate. Cook for 20-25 minutes. Serve. Enjoy!

Mezcal Shrimp With Salsa De Molcajete

Servings: 4
Cooking Time: 14 Minutes

Ingredients:

- 18 to 24 jumbo shrimp, about 1½lb (680g) total, peeled and deveined
- ⅓ cup mezcal
- juice of ½ lime
- 2 tbsp extra virgin olive oil
- 2 tsp coarse salt
- 1 tsp ground cumin
- lime wedges
- for the salsa
- 2 Roma tomatoes
- 2 tomatillos, husked and washed
- 2 garlic cloves, peeled and impaled on a toothpick
- 1 jalapeño or serrano pepper
- 1 small white onion, halved
- ½ tsp coarse salt, plus more
- juice of ½ lime
- ¼ cup loosely packed fresh cilantro leaves

Directions:

1. Supply your smoker with wood pellets and follow the start-up procedure. Preheat the grill, with the lid closed, to 450° F.
2. In a large bowl, combine the shrimp, mezcal, lime juice, olive oil, salt, and ground cumin. Toss with your hands to mix thoroughly. Set aside for 15 minutes and then toss once more.
3. Begin to make the salsa by placing the tomatoes, tomatillos, garlic, jalapeño, and onion on the grate. Grill until they begin to char, about 3 minutes for the garlic and about 6 to 8 minutes for the other vegetables, turning as needed. Transfer the vegetables to a rimmed sheet pan. Remove the skewers from the garlic. Let everything cool. Coarsely chop the vegetables and leave them in separate piles.
4. Place the garlic in the molcajete and add the salt. Mash the garlic to a purée using the temolote. Add the onion and grind it into the garlic paste. Stir in the jalapeño (deseeded for a milder salsa), tomatoes, and tomatillos. Stir in the lime juice and cilantro leaves. Taste, adding salt. (If you don't own a molcajete or temolote, prepare the salsa using a small food processor.)

5. Drain the shrimp and discard the marinade. Thread the shrimp on wood or bamboo skewers. Place the shrimp on the grate and grill until they're white and opaque, about 4 to 6 minutes, tossing with tongs.

6. Transfer the shrimp to a platter. Serve with the salsa and lime wedges.

Smoked Honey Salmon

Servings: 2
Cooking Time: 25 Minutes

Ingredients:

- 1 lb. salmon fillets
- 1/2 tsp. pepper
- 1/4 tsp. salt
- 2 tbsp. sriracha
- 2 tsp. honey
- 2 tsp. chili sauce
- 1 tsp. lime juice
- 1/2 tsp. fish sauce

Directions:

1. Supply your smoker with wood pellets and follow the start-up procedure. Preheat the grill, with the lid closed, to 350° F.

2. Sprinkle the salmon with salt and pepper.

3. In a bowl, whisk together the sriracha, honey, chili sauce, lime juice, and fish sauce.

4. Once the grill is hot, place the salmon on the grill and leave for 15 minutes.

5. After 15 minutes, brush the salmon with the sriracha chili sauce and keep cooking for 5-10minutes. The salmon should be firm to the touch and crispy on the edges.

6. Serve hot!

Lime Mahi Mahi Fillets

Servings: 4

Cooking Time: 8 Minutes

Ingredients:

- 3/4 cup extra-virgin olive oil
- 1 clove garlic, minced
- 1/8 teaspoon ground black pepper
- 1/2 teaspoon cayenne pepper
- 2 tablespoons dill weed.
- 1 pinch salt
- 2 tablespoons lime juice
- 1/8 teaspoon grated lime peel
- 2 (4 ounce) mahi mahi fillets

Directions:

1. Supply your smoker with wood pellets and follow the start-up procedure. Preheat the grill, with the lid closed, to 325° F.

2. Lightly oil the grate.

3. Combine in a bowl the extra-virgin olive oil, minced garlic, black pepper, cayenne pepper, salt, lime juice, and grated lime zest.

4. Wisk to prepare the marinade.

5. Place the mahi mahi fillets in the marinade and turn to coat.

6. Allow to marinate at least 15 minutes.

7. Cook on preheated grill until fish flakes easily with a fork and is lightly browned (Typically 3 to 4 minutes per side).

8. Garnish with the twists of lime zest to serve.

Wood-fired Halibut

Servings: 4
Cooking Time: 20 Minutes

Ingredients:

- 1 pound halibut fillet
- 1 batch Dill Seafood Rub

Directions:

1. Supply your smoker with wood pellets and follow the start-up procedure. Preheat the grill, with the lid closed, to 325°F.

2. Sprinkle the halibut fillet on all sides with the rub. Using your hands, work the rub into the meat.

3. Place the halibut directly on the grill grate and grill until its internal temperature reaches 145°F. Remove the halibut from the grill and serve immediately.

Smoked Lobster Scampi

Servings: 2

Cooking Time: 30 Minutes

Ingredients:

- 1 Lobster Tail
- 1 Handful Pasta, Angel Hair
- 2 Tablespoon butter
- 1 Teaspoon garlic, minced
- 1/2 Teaspoon lemon juice
- 2 Teaspoon Parmesan cheese, grated
- 2 Tablespoon Sun Dried Tomato Pesto
- fresh parsley

Directions:

1. Supply your smoker with wood pellets and follow the start-up procedure. Preheat the grill, with the lid closed, to 180° F.

2. Use kitchen shears to cut along the top of the lobster on both sides to expose the meat. Place the lobster directly on the grill for 20-25 minutes, depending on the size of the lobster. Grill: 180 ˚F

3. While lobster smokes, cook pasta according to packaged directions.

4. After 20-25 minutes, take lobster off the grill and remove the meat from the tail. Cut meat into chunks.

5. While the pasta is boiling, melt butter over medium high heat. Once butter starts to brown, add the garlic and lobster chunks. Toss in pan a few times then add lemon and parmesan. Set aside.

6. When pasta has finished, place 1 tbsp of the sun dried tomato pesto on the bottom of a bowl or plate. Top with pasta, then finish with the lobster scampi. Garnish with parsley. Enjoy!

Garlic Grilled Shrimp Skewers

Servings: 3

Cooking Time: 6 Minutes

Ingredients:

- 1 pound large shrimp
- 1/4 cup olive oil
- 1/4 cup fresh cilantro, finely chopped
- 1/4 cup fresh parsley, finely chopped
- 4 cloves garlic, minced
- 1 tablespoon lemon juice
- 1/2 teaspoon salt
- 1/4 teaspoon black pepper
- Pinch cayenne pepper, adjust to spice preference

Directions:

1. Add the olive oil, herbs, and spices to a small mixing bowl and whisk together.

2. Place the shrimp in a bowl and pour 3/4 of the marinade on top of the shrimp. Mix together gently to coat the shrimp evenly.

3. Cover the bowl and marinate the shrimp for 30 minutes to an hour.

4. Thread the shrimp on the skewers and make sure to get all the good garlic and herbs from the bowl and spread on to the shrimp.

5. Supply your smoker with wood pellets and follow the start-up procedure. Preheat the grill, with the lid closed, to medium high heat.

6. Once the grill is hot, arrange the shrimp skewers on the grill and cook for 2-3 minutes per side, or until they turn pink and opaque.

7. Remove the shrimp skewers to a plate and spoon the remaining marinade on top before serving.

Moules Marinières With Garlic Butter Sauce

Servings: 4
Cooking Time: 12 Minutes

Ingredients:

- 3lb (1.4kg) fresh mussels, scrubbed under cold running water and debearded
- lemon wedges
- crusty bread (optional)
- for the sauce
- 6 tbsp unsalted butter
- 3 garlic cloves, peeled and minced
- 1 cup dry white wine or hard cider
- 1 tbsp freshly squeezed lemon juice
- 2 tsp hot sauce, plus more
- coarse salt
- freshly ground black pepper
- 2 tbsp chopped fresh curly parsley or tarragon

Directions:

1. Supply your smoker with wood pellets and follow the start-up procedure. Preheat the grill, with the lid closed, to 450° F.

2. In a small saucepan on the stovetop over medium-low heat, make the sauce by melting the butter. Add the garlic and sauté for 1 to 2 minutes. Add the wine, lemon juice, and hot sauce. Season with salt and pepper to taste.

Simmer for 5 minutes. Remove the saucepan from the heat and stir in the parsley. Keep warm.

3. Discard any mussels that are cracked or don't snap shut when tapped. Place the mussels in a large aluminum foil roasting pan and cover tightly with heavy-duty aluminum foil.

4. Place the pan on the grate and steam the mussels until the shells open, about 10 to 12 minutes. Remove the pan from the grill and use long-handled tongs to remove the foil from the pan. (Be careful of escaping steam.) Use the tongs to discard any mussels that don't open.

5. Pour the reserved garlic butter sauce over the mussels. Serve from the pan or transfer the mussels to a shallow serving bowl. Serve immediately with lemon wedges, additional hot sauce, and crusty bread (if using) to sop up the juices.

Honey Balsamic Salmon

Servings: 2
Cooking Time: 25 Minutes

Ingredients:

- 1 Medium salmon fillet
- Fin & Feather Rub
- 1/2 Cup balsamic vinegar
- 1 Tablespoon minced garlic
- 2 Tablespoon honey

Directions:

1. Season the fillet with the Traeger Fin & Feather Rub.

2. Make the glaze: Combine the vinegar, garlic and honey in a small saucepan. Simmer over medium heat until reduced by half. Usually 10 to 15 minutes. The glaze will be properly reduced when it coats the back of a spoon. Using a basting brush, coat the fillet with the glaze.

3. Supply your smoker with wood pellets and follow the start-up procedure. Preheat the grill, with the lid closed, to 350° F.

4. Arrange the salmon fillet on the grill grate. Grill for 25 to 30 minutes, or until the salmon is opaque and flakes easily with a fork. Grill: 350 ˚F

5. Transfer to a platter or plates and serve immediately. If desired, heat any remaining glaze to a boil and drizzle over top of the salmon. Enjoy!

Oysters Margarita

Servings: 4
Cooking Time: 10minutes

Ingredients:

- 24 fresh oysters in the shell
- 4oz (120ml) freshly squeezed lime juice
- 2oz (60ml) tequila
- 2oz (60ml) orange liqueur, such as triple sec
- 6 tbsp cold butter, cut into 24 cubes
- crunchy salt, such as margarita rimming salt
- lime wedges
- hot sauce (optional)

Directions:

1. Supply your smoker with wood pellets and follow the start-up procedure. Preheat the grill, with the lid closed, to 450° F.

2. Carefully shuck each oyster to remove the top shell. Run your shucking knife under the oyster to release it from the bottom shell, but don't spill the juices. Discard the top shells, but keep the oysters in the bottom shells. Balance each oyster on a wire rack placed on a rimmed sheet pan.

3. Place 1 teaspoon of lime juice, ½ teaspoon of tequila, ½ teaspoon of orange liqueur, and 1 cube of butter on each oyster.

4. Place the pan on the grate and smoke until the butter has melted and the juices are bubbling, about 8 to 10 minutes. (The oysters should be just barely cooked.)

5. Remove the pan from the grill. Sprinkle a pinch of salt on each oyster. Serve immediately with lime wedges and hot sauce (if using).

Delicious Smoked Trout

Servings: 8
Cooking Time: 120 Minutes

Ingredients:

- 6 rainbow trout fillets
- Brine:
- 2 Tablespoons kosher salt
- 2 Tablespoons brown sugar
- 4 cups cool water

Directions:

1. For the brine, dissolve the kosher salt and brown sugar in water.

2. Place the trout fillets in the brine, skin side up, and brine the fillets for 15 minutes.

3. Supply your smoker with wood pellets and follow the start-up procedure. Preheat the grill, with the lid closed, to 180° F.

4. Remove the trout from the brine and transfer it to the grill grates.

5. Smoke the trout for 1.5 to 2 hours with the lid closed, depending on the thickness of your fillets.

6. Smoke until the trout reaches an internal temperature of 145 ˚F, or until the trout flakes easily.

7. Remove the trout from the smoker and serve warm, or let it cool completely and serve chilled with your favorite accouterments.

Roasted Halibut With Spring Vegetables

Servings: 4

Cooking Time: 20 Minutes

Ingredients:

- 4 thick-cut halibut fillets
- 2 Tablespoon Fin & Feather Rub
- Butcher Paper
- 1 Pound Carrots, Peeled and Cut into 3/4" Inch Slices
- 1 Pound asparagus, ends trimmed
- 1/2 Pound Oyster Mushrooms
- 2 Tablespoon butter
- salt and pepper
- 1/2 Cup white wine

Directions:

1. Season the halibut fillets with Traeger Fin and Feather Rub.

2. To build the packets: Start with four sheets of parchment paper about twenty inches long. Fold in half, then open it back up.

3. Divide the carrots, asparagus, and mushrooms between the four pieces of parchment and top each with a little bit of butter. Season with salt and pepper. Place a halibut fillet on top of the vegetables in each packet.

4. Next, fold the paper over so the two ends meet, enclosing the food. Beginning at either end of the center crease, make small, overlapping diagonal folds around the filling, sealing the packet tight. Before finishing the final fold, pour a little bit of wine in each packet then seal completely.

5. Supply your smoker with wood pellets and follow the start-up procedure. Preheat the grill, with the lid closed, to 500° F.

6. Place all four packets on a sheet tray and place in the grill. Cook for 7-10 minutes or until the internal temperature of the fish reaches 145°F. Remove from the grill and place packet on a serving dish. Grill: 500 °F Probe: 145 °F

7. Using a knife or scissors, cut open each packet and fold the edges back. Finish with a little bit of lemon juice if desired. Enjoy!

Oysters In The Shell

Servings: 4

Cooking Time: 20 Minutes

Ingredients:

- 8 medium oysters, unopened, in the shell, rinsed and scrubbed
- 1 batch Lemon Butter Mop for Seafood

Directions:

1. Supply your smoker with wood pellets and follow the start-up procedure. Preheat the grill, with the lid closed, to 375°F.

2. Place the unopened oysters directly on the grill grate and grill for about 20 minutes, or until the oysters are done and their shells open.

3. Discard any oysters that do not open. Shuck the remaining oysters, transfer them to a bowl, and add the mop. Serve immediately.

Garlic Pepper Shrimp Pesto Bruschetta

Servings: 12

Cooking Time: 15 Minutes

Ingredients:

- 12 Slices Bread, Baguette
- 1/2 Tsp Chili Pepper Flakes
- 1/2 Tsp Garlic Powder
- 4 Cloves Garlic, Minced

- 2 Tbsp Olive Oil
- 1/2 Tsp Paprika, Smoked
- 1/4 Tsp Parsley, Leaves
- Pepper
- Pesto
- Salt
- 12 Shrimp, Jumbo

Directions:

1. Supply your smoker with wood pellets and follow the start-up procedure. Preheat the grill, with the lid closed, to 350° F. Place the baguette slices on a baking sheet lined with foil. Stir together the olive oil, and minced garlic, then brush both sides of the baguette slices with the mix. Place the pan inside the grill, and bake for about 10-15 minutes.

2. In a skillet, add a splash of olive oil, shrimp, chili powder, garlic powder, smoked paprika, salt pepper, and grill on medium-high heat for about 5 minutes (until the shrimp is pink). Be sure to stir often. Once pink, remove pan from heat. Once the baguettes are toasted, let them cool for 5 minutes, then spread a layer of pesto onto each one, then top with a shrimp, and serve.

Grilled Lemon Salmon

Servings: 4
Cooking Time: 60 Minutes

Ingredients:
- Dill, Fresh
- 1 Lemon, Sliced
- 1 1/2 - 2 Lbs Salmon, Fresh

Directions:

1. Supply your smoker with wood pellets and follow the start-up procedure. Preheat the grill, with the lid closed, to 225° F.

2. Place the salmon on a cedar plank. Lay the lemon slices along the top of the salmon. Smoke in your Grill for about 60 minutes.

3. Top with fresh dill and serve.

Flavour Fire Spiced Shrimp

Servings: 2
Cooking Time: 8 Minutes

Ingredients:
- 1 pound of extra large raw whole wild shrimp
- 1 tablespoon vegetable oil
- 1 tablespoon chili powder
- 1 teaspoon garlic powder
- 1/2 teaspoon onion powder
- 1/2 teaspoon cayenne pepper
- 1/4 teaspoon paprika
- 1/4 teaspoon dried oregano
- Pinch of Kosher salt

Directions:

1. Supply your smoker with wood pellets and follow the start-up procedure. Preheat the grill, with the lid closed, to High heat.

2. While grill is preheating, remove the shrimp shells, leaving the heads.

3. Butterfly shrimp by using a knife to cut each shrimp down the middle, from the head down to the tail.

4. Remove the vein, rinse off the shrimp and lightly dry off with paper towels.

5. Place the shrimp in a large bowl, sprinkle with all the seasonings and the oil.

6. Mix together, ensuring the mixture evenly covers each shrimp.

7. Using a skewer, impale the whole body of a shrimp, from head to tail. (Wrap them in aluminum foil if using wooden skewers).

8. Place the whole shrimp on the grill and cook for 3-4 minutes on each side (Or until shells turns pink and the shrimp is opaque).

9. Serve with your favorite sauce or condiment.

Cajun-blackened Shrimp

Servings: 4

Cooking Time: 20 Minutes

Ingredients:

- 1 pound peeled and deveined shrimp, with tails on
- 1 batch Cajun Rub
- 8 tablespoons (1 stick) butter
- ¼ cup Worcestershire sauce

Directions:

1. Supply your smoker with wood pellets and follow the start-up procedure. Preheat the grill, with the lid closed, to 450°F and place a cast-iron skillet on the grill grate. Wait about 10 minutes after your grill has reached temperature, allowing the skillet to get hot.

2. Meanwhile, season the shrimp all over with the rub.

3. When the skillet is hot, place the butter in it to melt. Once the butter melts, stir in the Worcestershire sauce.

4. Add the shrimp and gently stir to coat. Smoke-braise the shrimp for about 10 minutes per side, until opaque and cooked through. Remove the shrimp from the grill and serve immediately.

Smoked Crab Legs

Servings: 4

Cooking Time: 30 Minutes

Ingredients:

- 4 Whole crab legs
- 4 Tablespoon butter, melted
- 1/2 Cup Texas Spicy BBQ Sauce
- salt and pepper
- 1 Tablespoon Fin & Feather Rub

Directions:

1. Supply your smoker with wood pellets and follow the start-up procedure. Preheat the grill, with the lid closed, to 250° F.

2. Place the crab legs directly on the grill grate and smoke for 20 minutes. Grill: 250 °F

3. While the crab is smoking, make the sauce. In a medium bowl, combine melted butter, Traeger Texas Spicy BBQ sauce, salt, pepper and Traeger Fin & Feather Rub.

4. After 20 minutes of cooking, brush the crab legs with the BBQ sauce mixture. Continue to cook for another 10 minutes reserving the remaining sauce to serve. Remove crab legs from the grill, and serve with melted butter and BBQ sauce mixture. Enjoy!

Grilled Tuna Steaks With Lemon & Caper Butter

Servings: 4

Cooking Time: 8 Minutes

Ingredients:

- 4 tuna steaks, each about 8oz (225g) and 1 inch (2.5cm) thick
- extra virgin olive oil
- coarse salt
- freshly ground black pepper
- for the butter
- 6 tbsp unsalted butter, chilled, divided
- 1 garlic clove, peeled and minced
- 3 tbsp brined capers, drained and coarsely chopped
- 1 tbsp freshly squeezed lemon juice, plus more

- 1 tsp lemon zest
- 1 tbsp minced fresh chives or flat-leaf parsley

Directions:

1. Supply your smoker with wood pellets and follow the start-up procedure. Preheat the grill, with the lid closed, to 450° F.

2. In a small saucepan on the stovetop over medium-low heat, begin making the butter by melting 1 tablespoon of butter. (Cut the remaining butter into ½-inch (1.25cm) cubes and keep them cold.) Add the garlic and capers. Cook until the garlic is softened, about 3 minutes. Stir in the lemon juice and zest. Remove the saucepan from the heat and set aside.

3. Lightly brush the tuna steaks with olive oil. Season with salt and pepper. Place the steaks on the grate and grill until seared, about 3 to 4 minutes per side. (The tuna will be quite rare in the center, almost like sashimi. If you prefer your tuna more well done, add 4 to 6 minutes to the grilling time.)

4. Transfer the steaks to a platter and let rest for 5 minutes.

5. Reheat the butter and caper mixture over low heat. Whisk in the chilled butter one or two cubes at a time until the sauce has emulsified. Stir in the chives. Ladle the sauce over the tuna. Serve immediately.

Grilled Lemon Lobster Tails

Servings: 3
Cooking Time: 7 Minutes

Ingredients:

- 6 lobster tails
- 1/4 cup melted butter
- 1/4 cup fresh lemon juice
- 1 tablespoon fresh dill
- 1 teaspoon salt
- 6 lime wedges

Directions:

1. Supply your smoker with wood pellets and follow the start-up procedure. Preheat the grill, with the lid closed, to 375° F.

2. Split the lobster tails in half place then back side down.

3. Cut down through the center to the shell the whole length of each tail.

4. Pull the shell back, exposing the meat.

5. Pat the lobster tails with paper towel to dry.

6. Combine in a small mixing bowl the butter, lemon juice, dill, and salt until the salt has dissolved.

7. Brush the mixture onto the flesh side of each lobster tail.

8. Place the lobster tails onto the grill and cook for 5 to 7 minutes, turning them once during the cooking process. (The shells should turn a bright pink).

9. Remove the heat.

10. Serve with lime wedges!

Spicy Crab Poppers

Servings: 8
Cooking Time: 30 Minutes

Ingredients:

- 18 Whole jalapeño
- 8 Ounce cream cheese, softened
- 1 Cup Canned Corn, drained
- 1/2 Cup Crab meat, lump
- 1 1/4 Teaspoon Old Bay Seasoning
- 2 Scallions, minced

Directions:

1. Cut each jalapeño in half lengthwise through the stem and remove the ribs and seeds.

2. Filling: In a mixing bowl, combine the cream cheese, corn, crab meat, scallions, and Old Bay Seasoning and stir until blended. Stir in the scallions. Spoon the filling into the jalapeño halves, mounding it slightly.

3. Arrange the poppers on a baking sheet covered with foil or parchment paper.

4. Supply your smoker with wood pellets and follow the start-up procedure. Preheat the grill, with the lid closed, to 350° F.

5. Roast the jalapeños for 25 to 30 minutes, or until the peppers have softened and the filling is hot and bubbling.

6. Let cool slightly before serving. Enjoy!

Cold-smoked Salmon Gravlax

Servings: 6
Cooking Time: 30 Minutes

Ingredients:
- 1 Cup kosher salt
- 1 Cup sugar
- 1 Tablespoon freshly ground black pepper
- 2 Pound Sushi-Grad Salmon Fillet, Skin-on, Pin Bones Removed
- 2 Bunch Dill Weed, fresh
- capers, drained
- red onion, sliced
- cream cheese
- lemons

Directions:
1. In a bowl stir together the salt, sugar and black pepper until thoroughly combined. On a work surface, turn salmon skin side up and sprinkle about half of salt mixture all over and rub in.

2. Arrange half the dill on the bottom of a baking dish large enough to hold the salmon. Set salmon skin side down on bed of dill.

3. Rub remaining salt mixture all over top and sides of salmon, then top with remaining dill. Cover with plastic, then top with a weight on a smaller baking dish or a plate with cans of beans on top, then place in refrigerator and allow to cure for 2 days.

4. Remove salmon from refrigerator, rinse under cold water and pat dry with paper towels. Allow to sit at room temperature on the counter for 1 hour

5. Supply your smoker with wood pellets and follow the start-up procedure. Preheat the grill, with the lid closed, to 180° F. Place salmon onto a baking pan. Fill another baking pan with ice and place baking pan with salmon over ice. Place onto grill and smoke for 30 minutes.

6. Remove from grill and slice thin. Serve with capers, red onion, dill, cream cheese, and lemon. Enjoy!

Smoked Sugar Halibut

Servings: 8
Cooking Time: 120 Minutes

Ingredients:
- 1/4 cup granulated sugar
- 1/4 cup brown sugar
- 1/2 cup kosher salt
- 1 tsp ground coriander
- 2 lbs fresh halibut

Directions:
1. In a small bowl, mix the sugars, salt,and coriander together. Season the halibut on all sides.

2. Wrap the halibut in plastic wrap, place on a rimmed sheet pan,and brine in the fridge for 3 hours.

3. Remove the plastic wrap and rinse the fish. Pat it dry. Set it on a drying rack over a sheet pan for 1-2 hours in the fridge.

4. Supply your smoker with wood pellets and follow the start-up procedure. Preheat the grill, with the lid closed, to 200° F. Smoke the fish for 2 hours or until its internal temperature reaches 140 °F.

5. Serve your preferred sauce with the fish.

Barbecued Shrimp

Servings: 4
Cooking Time: 10 Minutes

Ingredients:
- 1 pound peeled and deveined shrimp, with tails on
- 2 tablespoons olive oil
- 1 batch Dill Seafood Rub

Directions:
1. Soak wooden skewers in water for 30 minutes.
2. Supply your smoker with wood pellets and follow the start-up procedure. Preheat the grill, with the lid closed, to 375°F.
3. Thread 4 or 5 shrimp per skewer.
4. Coat the shrimp all over with olive oil and season each side of the skewers with the rub.
5. Place the skewers directly on the grill grate and grill the shrimp for 5 minutes per side. Remove the skewers from the grill and serve immediately.

Grilled Maple Syrup Salmon

Servings: 6
Cooking Time: 30 Minutes

Ingredients:
- 1 large salmon fillet (around 3 pounds)
- 1/2 cup salted butter (melted)
- 2 tablespoons soy sauce
- Salt and pepper
- 1/4 cup maple syrup

Directions:
1. Supply your smoker with wood pellets and follow the start-up procedure. Preheat the grill, with the lid closed, to 400° F.
2. Place the salmon fillet in a baking pan lined with parchment paper.
3. Sprinkle the fish with salt and pepper.
4. Add half of the melted butter to the salmon and place the baking pan on the grill.
5. Grill for 15-20 minutes or until fish is roughly 70% cooked. It will feel still gelatinous in the thickest parts of the salmon.
6. Combine the remaining melted butter, soy sauce, and maple syrup and pour over the salmon.It will run off the sides so use a spoon to pour it back over the fish. It's also perfectly fine that some will be left on the sides of the pan.
7. Cook for 5 to 10 additional minutes or until the fish is cooked through. The fish should be firm to the touch but still moist and soft when pressed on,and the ridges will flake or pull apart if pressed on.

Garlic Blackened Catfish

Servings: 4
Cooking Time: 10 Minutes

Ingredients:
- ½ Cup Cajun Seasoning
- ¼ Tsp Cayenne Pepper
- 1 Tsp Granulated Garlic
- 1 Tsp Ground Thyme

- 1 Tsp Onion Powder
- 1 Tsp Ground Oregano
- 1 Tsp Pepper
- 4 (5-Oz.) Skinless Catfish Fillets
- 1 Tbsp Smoked Paprika
- 1 Stick Unsalted Butter

Directions:

1. In a small bowl, combine the Cajun seasoning, smoked paprika, onion powder, granulated garlic, ground oregano, ground thyme, pepper and cayenne pepper.

2. Sprinkle fish with salt and let rest for 20 minutes.

3. Supply your smoker with wood pellets and follow the start-up procedure. Preheat the grill, with the lid closed, to 450° F. If you're using a gas or charcoal grill, set it up for medium-high heat. Place cast iron skillet on the grill and let it preheat.

4. While grill is preheating, sprinkle catfish fillets with seasoning mixture, pressing gently to adhere. Add half the butter to preheated cast iron skillet and swirl to coat, add more butter if needed. Place fillets in hot skillet and cook 3-5 minutes or until a dark crust has been formed. Flip and cook an additional 3-5 minutes or until the fish flakes apart when pressed gently with your finger.

5. Remove fish from grill and sprinkle evenly with fresh parsley. Serve with lemon wedges and enjoy!

VEGETABLES RECIPES

Smoked Jalapeño Poppers

Servings: 4
Cooking Time: 60 Minutes

Ingredients:

- 12 Medium jalapeño
- 6 Slices bacon, cut in half
- 8 Ounce cream cheese
- 2 Tablespoon Pork & Poultry Rub
- 1 Cup grated cheese

Directions:

1. Supply your smoker with wood pellets and follow the start-up procedure. Preheat the grill, with the lid closed, to 180° F. For optimal flavor, use Super Smoke if available.

2. Slice the jalapeños in half lengthwise. Scrape out any seeds and ribs with a small spoon or paring knife. Mix softened cream cheese with Traeger Pork & Poultry rub and grated cheese. Spoon mixture onto each jalapeño half. Wrap with bacon and secure with a toothpick.

3. Place the jalapeños on a rimmed baking sheet. Place on grill and smoke for 30 minutes. Grill: 180 ˚F

4. Increase the grill temperature to 375˚F and cook an additional 30 minutes or until bacon is cooked to desired doneness. Serve warm, enjoy! Grill: 375 ˚F

Roasted Pumpkin Seeds

Servings: 8
Cooking Time: 40 Minutes

Ingredients:

- 1 Whole Pumpkin, seeds

- olive oil or vegetable oil
- Jacobsen Salt Co. Pure Kosher Sea Salt

Directions:

1. As soon as possible after removing the seeds from the pumpkin, rinse pumpkin seeds under cold water in a colander and pick out the pulp and strings.

2. Place the pumpkin seeds in a single layer on an oiled baking sheet, stirring to coat. Supply your smoker with wood pellets and follow the start-up procedure. Preheat the grill, with the lid closed, to 180° F.

3. Place the baking sheet with the seeds on the grill grate, close the lid, and smoke for 20 minutes. Grill: 180 ˚F

4. Sprinkle your seeds with salt and turn the temperature on your grill up to 325˚F. Roast the seeds until toasted, about 20 minutes. Check and stir seeds after the first 10 minutes. Grill: 325 ˚F

5. Seeds will be brown because they were smoked before being roasted. Enjoy!

Red Potato Grilled Lollipops

Servings: 4
Cooking Time: 25 Minutes

Ingredients:

- 8 Large red bliss potatoes, halved
- 2 Clove garlic, minced
- 2 Sprig rosemary, minced
- 2 Tablespoon olive oil
- 1 Teaspoon salt
- 1/2 Teaspoon black pepper
- 5 Wooden Skewers, soaked in water
- 1/4 Cup Parmesan cheese, grated

Directions:

1. Supply your smoker with wood pellets and follow the start-up procedure. Preheat the grill, with the lid closed, to 450° F.

2. Halve potatoes and poke each several times with a fork.

3. Put the potatoes in a large bowl and toss with the minced garlic, rosemary leaves, a few tablespoons of olive oil, kosher salt, and pepper. Microwave the potatoes for 4 minutes. Gently toss potatoes and microwave for another 3 minutes.

4. Skewer potato halves threading about 4 or 5 potato halves on each skewer. Brush potatoes with olive oil.

5. Place the potato skewers on the Traeger, cut side down, and grill until the sides begin to brown (4-7 minutes).

6. Flip and grill skin side down for another 7-10 minutes.

7. They are done when a sharp knife tip easily penetrates the sides. Remove potatoes from grill and top with grated parmesan cheese. Enjoy!

Baked Loaded Tater Tots

Servings: 6
Cooking Time: 35 Minutes

Ingredients:
- 2 Pound frozen tater tots
- 1 Can Black Beans
- 1 1/2 Cup leftover chili
- 1 Cup leftover queso
- 1 red onion, finely diced
- 1/2 Cup chopped cilantro
- 1/2 Cup sour cream
- 1 jalapeños, sliced

Directions:

1. Supply your smoker with wood pellets and follow the start-up procedure. Preheat the grill, with the lid closed, to 375° F.

2. Spread frozen tots out on a sheet tray and place directly on the grill grate.

3. Cook for 20 to 25 minutes or until tots are crispy. Grill: 375 ℉

4. Top with warmed chili, queso and beans. Place back on the grill for 15 minutes. Grill: 375 ℉

5. Remove from grill and top with red onion, cilantro, sour cream and jalapeño. Enjoy!

Roasted Vegetable Napoleon

Servings: 4
Cooking Time: 30 Minutes

Ingredients:
- 2 Whole sweet potatoes
- 2 Whole zucchini
- 2 Whole Squash
- 1 Whole red onion
- 2 Whole Bell Pepper, Red
- salt and pepper

Directions:

1. Supply your smoker with wood pellets and follow the start-up procedure. Preheat the grill, with the lid closed, to High heat.

2. Salt and pepper all vegetables and grill them on both sides. Begin with the peppers and onions as they will take a little longer to cook. Grill: 450 ℉

Smoked Mashed Potatoes

Servings: 6

Cooking Time: 45 Minutes

Ingredients:

- 2 Pound red bliss potatoes, washed and diced medium
- chicken stock or water
- 1/2 Stick salted butter
- 1 Cup whole milk
- 1/2 Cup sour cream
- 1/2 Cup shredded or grated Parmesan cheese
- kosher salt
- freshly ground black pepper
- 1/2 Cup fresh sliced green onions

Directions:

1. Place the diced red potatoes into a small saucepan or stockpot and cover with chicken stock or water.

2. Bring to a boil and cook on a simmer until fork tender, then cook 4 to 5 minutes past that until soft.

3. Supply your smoker with wood pellets and follow the start-up procedure. Preheat the grill, with the lid closed, to 400° F.

4. In a separate ovenproof pan, such as a cast iron skillet, add butter and milk and place in the Traeger during start up, until melted (approximately 7 to 10 minutes). Grill: 400 ℉

5. Carefully remove the butter/milk mixture from the Traeger using heatproof gloves.

6. Drain the potatoes and place into a large bowl. Add the melted butter/milk mixture and slowly mash.

7. Add sour cream, cheese and green onions, then season to taste with salt and pepper.

8. Place into the cast iron skillet, then place the skillet back into the Traeger and cook until the potatoes have a slight crust and are bubbling, about 15 minutes. Grill: 400 ℉

9. Carefully remove the mashed potatoes from the Traeger using heatproof gloves. Allow to cool for 5 minutes. Scoop and enjoy!

Grilled Corn On The Cob With Parmesan And Garlic

Servings: 6

Cooking Time: 30 Minutes

Ingredients:

- 4 Tablespoon butter, melted
- 2 Clove garlic, minced
- salt and pepper
- 8 ears fresh corn
- 1/2 Cup shaved Parmesan
- 1 Tablespoon chopped parsley

Directions:

1. Supply your smoker with wood pellets and follow the start-up procedure. Preheat the grill, with the lid closed, to 450° F.

2. Place butter, garlic, salt and pepper in a medium bowl and mix well.

3. Peel back corn husks and remove the silk. Rub corn with half of the garlic butter mixture.

4. Close husks and place directly on the grill grate. Cook for 25 to 30 minutes, turning occasionally until corn is tender. Grill: 450 ℉

5. Remove from grill, peel and discard husks. Place corn on serving tray, drizzle with remaining butter and top with Parmesan and parsley.

Roasted Tomatoes

Servings: 2
Cooking Time: 180 Minutes

Ingredients:

- 3 Large ripe tomatoes
- 1/2 Tablespoon kosher salt
- 1 Teaspoon coarse ground black pepper
- 1/4 Teaspoon sugar
- 1/4 Teaspoon thyme or basil
- olive oil

Directions:

1. Line a rimmed baking sheet with parchment paper.
2. Supply your smoker with wood pellets and follow the start-up procedure. Preheat the grill, with the lid closed, to 225° F.
3. Remove the stem end from each tomato and cut the tomatoes into 1/2 inch thick slices.
4. Combine the salt, pepper, sugar and thyme or basil in a small bowl and mix.
5. Pour olive oil into the well of a dinner plate.
6. Dip one side of each tomato slice in the olive oil and arrange on the baking sheet. Dust the tomato slices with the seasoning mixture.
7. Arrange the pan directly on the grill grate and roast the tomatoes until the juices stop running and the edges have contracted, about 3 hours. Remove from grill and enjoy!

Grilled Street Corn

Servings: 6
Cooking Time: 10 Minutes

Ingredients:

- 6 ears corn, husked
- 1 As Needed extra-virgin olive oil
- 1/4 Cup mayonnaise
- 1 Tablespoon ancho or guajillo chile powder
- 1/2 Cup chopped cilantro, plus more for serving
- 1 lime, zested and juiced
- salt
- 1/2 Cup Cotija cheese
- 1 As Needed cilantro, finely chopped

Directions:

1. Supply your smoker with wood pellets and follow the start-up procedure. Preheat the grill, with the lid closed, to 450° F.
2. Brush corn with oil and place on grill, turning occasionally.
3. While corn is on the grill, mix mayonnaise with chile powder, cilantro, lime juice and zest in a bowl. Season with salt.
4. After about 10 minutes corn should be cooked through and slightly charred on the outside. Remove from grill.
5. Top corn with chile mayonnaise then sprinkle on the Cotija cheese and chopped cilantro. Enjoy!

Skillet Potato Cake

Servings: 4
Cooking Time: 40 Minutes

Ingredients:

- 8 Tablespoon butter, melted
- 2 Pound russet potatoes, peeled and thinly sliced
- 3 Tablespoon kosher salt
- 2 Tablespoon freshly ground black pepper
- thyme

Directions:

1. Supply your smoker with wood pellets and follow the start-up procedure. Preheat the grill, with the lid closed, to 375° F.

2. Brush the bottom of a cast iron skillet with part of the melted butter. Place potato slices vertically around the outer edges then fill in the middle in the same fashion.

3. Pour additional melted butter over the top of the layers and sprinkle with salt and pepper.

4. Place skillet in grill and cook for 35 to 40 minutes or until potatoes are fork tender and golden brown.

5. Garnish with a sprinkle of fresh thyme over the top of the potatoes. Enjoy!

Roasted Jalapeno Cheddar Deviled Eggs

Servings: 6
Cooking Time: 30 Minutes

Ingredients:

- 7 Eggs, hard boiled
- 3 Tablespoon mayonnaise
- 1 Teaspoon brown mustard
- 1 Teaspoon apple cider vinegar
- 1 Dash hot sauce
- 1 jalapeño pepper, seeded and minced
- salt and pepper
- 1/2 Cup shredded cheddar cheese
- paprika

Directions:

1. Supply your smoker with wood pellets and follow the start-up procedure. Preheat the grill, with the lid closed, to 180° F.

2. Place your eggs directly on the grill grate and smoke for 30 minutes.

3. Remove from the grill and allow the eggs to cool. Smoking the eggs will give them a slightly yellowed color, but an intense smoky flavor. If a classic white egg is your preference, then skip this step.

4. Slice the eggs lengthwise and scoop the egg yolks directly into a gallon zip top bag.

5. Add the mayo, mustard, vinegar, hot sauce, roasted jalapeños and salt and pepper to the bag.

6. Zip the bag closed and, using your hands, knead all of the ingredients together in the bag until completely smooth.

7. Squeeze the yolk mixture into one corner of the bag and then cut the corner off. Pipe the yolk mixture into the whites.

8. Sprinkle with the finely shredded cheddar or paprika and chill until you are ready to serve. Enjoy!

Grilled Asparagus And Spinach Salad

Servings: 8
Cooking Time: 10 Minutes

Ingredients:

- 4 Fluid Ounce apple cider vinegar
- 8 Fluid Ounce Honey Bourbon BBQ Sauce
- 2 Bunch asparagus, ends trimmed
- 3 Fluid Ounce extra-virgin olive oil
- 2 Ounce Beef Rub
- 24 Ounce Spinach, fresh
- 4 Ounce candied pecans
- 4 Ounce feta cheese

Directions:

1. Combine apple cider vinegar and Traeger Apricot BBQ Sauce to create salad dressing.

2. Supply your smoker with wood pellets and follow the start-up procedure. Preheat the grill, with the lid closed, to High heat.

3. Toss the asparagus with Olive Oil and the Beef Shake. Put asparagus in the Traeger Grilling Basket and move the basket to the grill grate.

4. Grill for about 10 minutes. Remove the asparagus once it is cooked. Grill: 350 °F

5. Place the hot asparagus right on top of the bowl of spinach.

6. Add candied pecans, feta cheese & salad dressing then toss and serve. Enjoy!

Grilled Beer Cabbage

Servings: 4
Cooking Time: 50 Minutes

Ingredients:

- 2 Cabbage, head
- 1 Tablespoon extra-virgin olive oil
- 1 Teaspoon salt
- 1 Teaspoon freshly ground black pepper
- 14 Fluid Ounce Guinness Extra Stout

Directions:

1. Clean and core cabbages. Drizzle with olive oil and salt and pepper. Rub into the cabbage.

2. Supply your smoker with wood pellets and follow the start-up procedure. Preheat the grill, with the lid closed, to 180° F.

3. Place cabbages directly on grill grate; smoke for 15 to 20 minutes. Remove from grill and thickly slice cabbage. Grill: 180 °F

4. Place sliced cabbage in cast-iron skillet. Pour beer over cabbage and return to grill.

5. Increase temperature to 375°F and cook for 30 minutes, or until cabbage has reached desired softness. Grill: 375 °F

6. Serve with corned beef. Enjoy!

Grilled Cabbage Steaks With Warm Bacon Vinaigrette

Servings: 4
Cooking Time: 10 Minutes

Ingredients:

- 3 Strips thick-cut lean bacon, cut into 1/4 inch strips
- 1 Large shallot, minced
- 2 Tablespoon sherry vinegar
- 1 Tablespoon whole grain mustard
- 1 Teaspoon chopped thyme
- 2 Tablespoon olive oil, plus more as needed
- 1 Head green cabbage, cut into 3/4 inch thick slices (about 6 steaks)
- salt and pepper

Directions:

1. Supply your smoker with wood pellets and follow the start-up procedure. Preheat the grill, with the lid closed, to 450° F.

2. For the Vinaigrette: In a large skillet, cook the bacon in 2 tablespoons olive oil over medium-high heat until browned and crisp. Remove bacon from heat and stir in the shallot, vinegar, mustard and thyme then set aside.

3. Brush cabbage steaks with olive oil and season with salt and pepper. Place cabbage steaks directly on grill grate and grill for 5 minutes per side. Grill: 450 °F

4. Remove cabbage steaks from grill and drizzle with bacon vinaigrette. Enjoy!

Grilled Broccoli Rabe

Servings: 4
Cooking Time: 10 Minutes

Ingredients:

- 4 Tablespoon extra-virgin olive oil
- 4 Bunch broccoli rabe or broccolini
- kosher salt
- 1 lemon, halved

Directions:

1. Supply your smoker with wood pellets and follow the start-up procedure. Preheat the grill, with the lid closed, to 450° F.

2. On a platter or in a mixing bowl, drizzle the olive oil over the broccoli rabe. Use your hands to mix thoroughly, coating the vegetables evenly with the oil. Season with sea salt.

3. Place the broccoli rabe in one layer directly on the lowest grill grate. Close the lid and cook for 5 to 10 minutes. You want there to be some color and slight char on the first side. Flip and cook for a few more minutes. Grill: 450 ˚F

4. Transfer the broccoli rabe to a serving platter and squeeze the juice of half a lemon evenly over the top.

5. Serve with more lemon wedges on the side. Enjoy!

Baked Bacon Green Bean Casserole

Servings: 6

Cooking Time: 50 Minutes

Ingredients:
- 1 1/2 Pound Green Beans, fresh
- 1 Can cream of mushroom soup
- 1/2 Cup milk
- 1/2 Teaspoon Worcestershire sauce
- 1/2 Teaspoon black pepper
- 2/3 Cup French's Original Crispy Fried Onions
- 8 Slices bacon
- 1/4 Cup red bell pepper, diced
- 2/3 French's Original Crispy Fried Onions

Directions:
1. In a mixing bowl, combine beans, soup, milk, Worcestershire sauce, black pepper, 2/3 cup of the onions, 6 of the slices of crumbled bacon, and red bell pepper. Transfer to a 1-1/2 quart casserole dish.

2. Supply your smoker with wood pellets and follow the start-up procedure. Preheat the grill, with the lid closed, to 350° F.

3. Cook casserole until the filling is hot and bubbling, 35 to 40 minutes. Grill: 350 ˚F

4. Top with remaining onions and the last 2 slices of crumbled bacon and cook for 5 to 10 minutes more, or until the onions are crisp and beginning to brown. Serve, enjoy! Grill: 350 ˚F

Baked Sweet Potatoes

Servings: 8

Cooking Time: 60 Minutes

Ingredients:
- 1 Cup butter, softened
- 1/4 Cup pure maple syrup
- 1/2 Teaspoon ground cinnamon
- 8 Medium sweet potatoes

Directions:
1. Make the Maple-Cinnamon Butter: In a mixing bowl, combine the butter, maple syrup, and cinnamon and whip with a wooden spoon. (Alternatively, blend the ingredients using a hand-held mixer or a stand mixer.) Transfer to a small bowl, cover, and chill until serving time.

2. Supply your smoker with wood pellets and follow the start-up procedure. Preheat the grill, with the lid closed, to 375° F. Arrange the sweet potatoes on the grill grate and bake until soft, 1 to 1-1/2 hours, depending on the size of the potatoes. Make a slit in the side of each, and squeeze the ends gently to fluff.

3. Serve hot with the Maple-Cinnamon Butter. Enjoy!

Smoked Pico De Gallo

Servings: 4
Cooking Time: 30 Minutes

Ingredients:

- 3 Cup diced Roma tomatoes
- 1 jalapeño, diced
- 1/2 red onion, diced
- 1/2 Bunch cilantro, finely chopped
- 2 lime, juiced
- salt
- olive oil

Directions:

1. Supply your smoker with wood pellets and follow the start-up procedure. Preheat the grill, with the lid closed, to 180° F.

2. Place the diced tomatoes on a small sheet pan spreading them into a thin layer. Place the sheet pan directly on the grill and smoke for 30 minutes. Grill: 180 °F

3. When the tomatoes are finished, toss all ingredients in a medium bowl and finish with lime juice, salt and olive oil to taste. Serve and enjoy!

Roasted Sheet Pan Vegetables

Servings: 4
Cooking Time: 25 Minutes

Ingredients:

- 1 Small head purple cauliflower, stemmed and cut into 2 inch florets
- 1 Small head yellow cauliflower, stemmed and cut into 2 inch florets
- 4 Cup butternut squash
- 2 Cup oyster or shiitake mushrooms, rinsed and sliced
- 3 Tablespoon olive oil
- 2 Teaspoon kosher salt
- freshly ground black pepper
- 1/4 Cup chopped flat-leaf parsley

Directions:

1. Supply your smoker with wood pellets and follow the start-up procedure. Preheat the grill, with the lid closed, to 450° F.

2. In a large mixing bowl, combine all of the vegetables. Drizzle olive oil over the top, along with kosher salt and a generous grinding of black pepper.

3. Using your hands, toss the vegetables until they are evenly coated.

4. Spread out onto 1 or 2 half sheet pans or baking sheets, ensuring there is a little space between the veggies. (If they are too crowded, the vegetables will steam instead of roast and you won't get that crispy texture.)

5. Place the sheet pans on the grill and cook for 15 minutes. Open and stir, then close the lid and continue to cook until the vegetables are brown around the edges, about 5 to 15 minutes longer. Grill: 450 °F

6. Toss with parsley and serve immediately. The vegetables are also delicious at room temperature. Enjoy!

Baked Heirloom Tomato Tart

Servings: 4
Cooking Time: 45 Minutes

Ingredients:

- 1 Whole Puff Pastry Sheet
- 2 Pound heirloom tomatoes, various shapes and sizes
- 1/2 Tablespoon kosher salt
- 1/2 Cup Ricotta Cheese
- 5 Whole eggs

- 1 To Taste salt and pepper
- 1/2 Teaspoon thyme leaves
- 1/2 Teaspoon red pepper flakes
- 4 Sprig thyme

Directions:

1. Supply your smoker with wood pellets and follow the start-up procedure. Preheat the grill, with the lid closed, to 350° F.

2. Place the puff pastry on a parchment lined sheet tray, and make a cut ¾ of the way through the pastry, ½" from the edge.

3. Slice the tomatoes and season with salt. Place on a sheet tray lined with paper towels.

4. In a small bowl combine the ricotta, 4 of the eggs, salt, thyme leaves, red pepper flakes and black pepper. Whisk together until combined. Spread the ricotta mixture over the puff pastry, staying within ½" from the edge.

5. In a small bowl whisk the last egg. Brush the egg wash onto the exposed edges of the pastry.

6. Place the sheet tray directly on the grill grate and bake for 45 minutes, rotating half-way through. Grill: 350 ˚F

7. When the edges are browned and the moisture from the tomatoes has evaporated, remove from the grill and let cool 5-7 minutes before serving. Enjoy!

Roasted Pickled Beets

Servings: 8
Cooking Time: 60 Minutes

Ingredients:

- 6 Medium Red Beets, scrubbed and trimmed
- 1 Cup red wine vinegar
- 1/2 Cup sugar
- 10 Whole peppercorns
- 1 Cup water

- 1 1/2 Teaspoon coarse salt
- 8 whole cloves
- 2 Pieces Star Anise, Broken
- 1 cinnamon stick, broken in half

Directions:

1. Make a foil pouch large enough to enclose the beets. Poke a few holes in the top to allow steam to escape.

2. Supply your smoker with wood pellets and follow the start-up procedure. Preheat the grill, with the lid closed, to 350° F.

3. Roast the beets until they are tender, 50 to 60 minutes. Carefully remove the foil and allow the beets to cool until they can be comfortably handled. Grill: 350 ˚F

4. Slip the skins off with your fingers. (You may wish to wear latex gloves to avoid staining your hands.) Cut the beets into quarters or slices. (Candy cane beets are especially pretty when sliced.)

5. In the meantime, make the brine: Bring the vinegar, sugar, salt, and water to a boil in a small saucepan over high heat.

6. Put the cloves, peppercorns, star anise, and cinnamon in a clean lidded jar, such as a canning jar

7. Add the beets to the jar. Pour the hot brine over the beets. Put the lid on the jar. Cool the beets to room temperature, then refrigerate for 3 to 5 days before serving. Enjoy!

Grilled Fingerling Potato Salad

Servings: 6
Cooking Time: 15 Minutes

Ingredients:

- 10 Whole scallions
- 2/3 Cup extra-virgin olive oil, divided

- 1 1/2 Pound fingerling potatoes, cut in half lengthwise
- pepper
- 2 Teaspoon kosher salt, divided, plus more as needed
- 2 Tablespoon rice vinegar
- 2 Teaspoon lemon juice
- 1 Small jalapeño, sliced

Directions:

1. Supply your smoker with wood pellets and follow the start-up procedure. Preheat the grill, with the lid closed, to 450° F.

2. Brush the scallions with oil and place on the grill.

3. Cook until lightly charred, about 2 to 3 minutes. Remove and let cool. Grill: 450 ˚F

4. Once the scallions have cooled, slice and set aside.

5. Brush the fingerling potatoes with oil (reserving 1/3 cup for later use), then salt and pepper. Place cut-side down on the grill until cooked through, about 4 to 5 minutes. Grill: 450 ˚F

6. In a bowl, whisk the remaining 1/3 cup olive oil, 1 teaspoon salt, rice vinegar and lemon juice. Next mix in the scallions, potatoes and sliced jalapeño.

7. Season with salt and pepper, and serve. Enjoy!

Portobello Marinated Mushroom

Servings: 2

Cooking Time: 15 Minutes

Ingredients:

- 1 Teaspoon chopped thyme
- 1 Teaspoon rosemary, chopped
- 1 Teaspoon Oregano, chopped
- 3 Tablespoon extra-virgin olive oil
- 1 To Taste Jacobsen Salt Co. Pure Kosher Sea Salt
- 1 To Taste pepper
- 6 Whole Portobello Mushroom
- 2 Whole russet potatoes

Directions:

1. Supply your smoker with wood pellets and follow the start-up procedure. Preheat the grill, with the lid closed, to 450° F.

2. Mix fresh herbs, olive oil, salt, and pepper together in a bowl. Rub over mushrooms. Grill both sides of mushrooms for approximately 2-3 minutes on each side. Grill: 450 ˚F

3. Clean the potatoes and slice into long strips.

4. Heat the oil on the Traeger in a sauce pan; drop the potatoes in the hot oil and fry for 7-8 minutes. Let the potatoes cool slightly on a sheet pan. Enjoy! Grill: 450 ˚F

Baked Kale Chips

Servings: 4

Cooking Time: 20 Minutes

Ingredients:

- 2 Bunch kale, leaves washed and stems removed
- 1 As Needed extra-virgin olive oil
- 1 To Taste sea salt

Directions:

1. Dry the kale leaves well and lay them out on a sheet tray. Drizzle lightly with olive oil and sprinkle with sea salt.

2. Supply your smoker with wood pellets and follow the start-up procedure. Preheat the grill, with the lid closed, to 250° F.

3. Place the sheet tray directly on the grill grate and cook until kale is lightly browned and crispy, about 20 minutes. Enjoy! Grill: 250 ˚F

Smoked Parmesan Herb Popcorn

Servings: 2

Cooking Time: 15 Minutes

Ingredients:

- 4 Tablespoon butter
- 2 Teaspoon Italian Seasoning
- 1 Teaspoon garlic powder
- 1 Teaspoon salt
- 1/4 Cup popcorn kernels
- 1/2 Cup Parmesan cheese, grated

Directions:

1. Supply your smoker with wood pellets and follow the start-up procedure. Preheat the grill, with the lid closed, to 250° F.

2. In a small saucepan, melt the butter over medium heat. Add Italian seasoning, garlic powder, and salt and stir to combine. Remove from heat and set aside.

3. Add 1/4 cup of popcorn to a brown paper lunch bag. Fold the top of the bag over twice to close. Place the bag in the microwave and microwave on high for 1 to 2 minutes, or until there are about 5 seconds between pops. Open the bag with care and dump into a large mixing bowl.

4. Pour butter mixture of popcorn in a bowl and toss to combine. Dump popcorn onto a baking sheet and place in grill.

5. Smoke for 10 minutes; remove from grill. Toss with parmesan cheese to serve. Enjoy! Grill: 250 °F

Roasted Do-ahead Mashed Potatoes

Servings: 6

Cooking Time: 50 Minutes

Ingredients:

- 5 Pound Yukon Gold or russet potatoes
- 9 Tablespoon butter
- 8 Ounce cream cheese
- 1/2 Cup milk
- salt and pepper

Directions:

1. Peel the potatoes and cut into chunks that are roughly the same size. Cover with cold water and add a teaspoon of salt. Bring to a boil over high heat, then reduce the heat to medium and simmer the potatoes until they are tender.

2. Drain the potatoes and return them to the pot. Stir over low heat for 2 to 3 minutes to evaporate any excess moisture.

3. Mash the potatoes with a hand-held potato masher. (Alternative, rice the potatoes using a ricer.) Incorporate 8 tbsp butter and cream cheese. Add milk until the potatoes are of a good consistency. Stir in salt and pepper to taste.

4. Butter the inside of a casserole dish. Spread the potatoes out in an even layer in the casserole dish, smoothing the top with a spatula. Cool, cover, and refrigerate if not cooking right away. Before cooking, let the potatoes warm to room temperature (about an hour).

5. Supply your smoker with wood pellets and follow the start-up procedure. Preheat the grill, with the lid closed, to 350° F.

6. Bake the potatoes for 45 to 50 minutes, or until hot through. Grill: 350 °F

PORK RECIPES

Grilled Bacon Dog

Servings: 4
Cooking Time: 25 Minutes

Ingredients:

- 16 hot dogs
- 16 Slices Bacon, sliced
- 2 Vidalia onion, sliced
- 16 hot dog buns
- 'Que BBQ Sauce
- Velveeta cheese

Directions:

1. Supply your smoker with wood pellets and follow the start-up procedure. Preheat the grill, with the lid closed, to 375° F.

2. Wrap bacon strips around the hot dogs, and grill directly on the grill grate for 10 minutes each side. Grill onions at the same time as the hot dogs, and cook for 10 -15 minutes.

3. Open hot dog buns and spread Traeger 'Que sauce, the grilled hot dogs, cheese sauce and grilled onions. Top with vegetables. Serve, enjoy!

Bangers And Potato Mash

Servings: 6 - 8
Cooking Time: 135 Minutes

Ingredients:

- Bbq Sauce
- ¼ Cup Butter
- 3 Garlic, Cloves
- 1 Onion, Chopped
- 8 Red Potatoes, Medium
- 8 Sausages, Pork
- ½ Cup Milk

Directions:

1. Using a fork, poke holes all over every red potato.

2. Cut a whole bulb of garlic in half and set aside.

3. Supply your smoker with wood pellets and follow the start-up procedure. Preheat the grill, with the lid open, to 300° F.

4. Set the halved garlic bulb and red potatoes on the grill. Cook the garlic for 30 minutes and the potatoes for 75 minutes.

5. Turn your down to 250°F and allow it to settle to that temperature.

6. Peel and mash the potatoes and garlic with butter and milk until the desired smoothness is achieved.

7. Set the sausages on the grill and smoke for 1 hour.

8. Sauté sliced onions in a pan with butter and barbecue sauce to taste.

9. After 1 hour, remove the sausages and turn off the grill. Place the onions on top of the mash potatoes and the sausage on top of the onions. Add more BBQ sauce if you wish.

Grilled Dr. Pepper Ribs

Servings: 4
Cooking Time: 300 Minutes

Ingredients:

- Aluminum Foil
- 2 Racks Baby Back Ribs
- 1 Cup Bbq Sauce
- 1 Stick Butter, Melted
- 1/2 Cup Dark Brown Sugar
- 12 Oz Dr. Pepper Soda

- 1/4 Cup Sweet Rib Rub
- 1/4 Cup Yellow Mustard

Directions:

1. Supply your smoker with wood pellets and follow the start-up procedure. Preheat the grill, with the lid open, to 225° F. If using a gas or charcoal grill, set it up for low, indirect heat.

2. After the grill comes to temp, place the ribs directly on the grill grates, close the lid, and smoke for 2 hours.

3. In a glass measuring cup, whisk together butter, brown sugar, and 8 ounces of Dr. Pepper.

4. Pour half of the mixture on a foil-lined sheet tray.

5. Place ribs, meat-side down, on top of the mixture, then pour remaining mixture on the bone-side. Tent the sheet tray with foil, then return to the grill for another 2 hours.

6. Remove ribs from liquid and set meat-side up directly on the grill grate.

7. Whisk together BBQ sauce and 4 ounces of Dr. Pepper, then brush half of the sauce all over the ribs.

8. Increase temperature to 275°F and cook an additional 30 to 60 minutes until ribs are tender, and meat pulls away from the bones.

9. Place ribs on a sheet tray, allow to rest for 10 minutes, then slice and serve with remaining BBQ sauce.

Grilled Pork Loin

Servings: 4
Cooking Time: 30 Minutes

Ingredients:

- 2 Tablespoons Balsamic Vinegar
- 2 Cups Fresh Washed And Dried Blackberries
- ¼ Cup Seedless Blackberry Preserve
- ½ Teaspoon Dijon Mustard
- Pinch Of Kosher Salt
- 1 Tablespoon Olive Oil
- 1 Pound Silver Skin And Extra Fat Removed Pork Loin
- 2 Tablespoons Sweet Rib Rub
- 1 Tablespoon Worcestershire Sauce

Directions:

1. Place your pork loin on a flat work surface. Trim the pork loin if necessary. Rub the tenderloin all over with olive oil until it is fully coated. Once the pork loin is completely coated, generously season all over with Sweet Rib Rub until every part of the pork loin is coated. Allow the pork tenderloin to rest at room temperature for 30 minutes.

2. While the pork loin rests, make the blackberry sauce. In a small bowl, place a metal strainer on top combine the fresh blackberries, seedless blackberry preserves, balsamic vinegar, Worcestershire sauce, Dijon mustard, and Sweet Rib Rub. Mix well and set aside.

3. Supply your smoker with wood pellets and follow the start-up procedure. Preheat the grill, with the lid open, to 350° F. If you're using a gas or charcoal grill, set it up for medium heat. Insert a temperature probe into the thickest part of the pork loin and smoke at 225°F for 4-5 hours, flipping once, until the pork loin is golden brown and charred in some spots, and reaches an internal temperature of 145°-165°F. Remove the pork loin from the grill and allow it to rest for 5 minutes.

4. Slice the pork loin thinly and serve with the blackberry sauce.

Unique Carolina Mustard Ribs

Servings: 4

Cooking Time: 300 Minutes

Ingredients:

- 1 Rack St. Louis Style Ribs
- 2 Cups Apple Juice
- 1/4 Cup Cider Vinegar
- 1/4 Cup Dark Brown Sugar
- 1/4 Cup Honey
- 1 Tablespoon Hot Sauce
- 2 Tablespoons Ketchup
- 7 Tablespoon Sweet Rib Rub
- 1 Tablespoon Worcestershire Sauce
- 2 Cups, Prepared Yellow Mustard

Directions:

1. Make the sauce for the ribs. In a large mixing bowl, combine 1 cup of the yellow mustard, cider vinegar, dark brown sugar, honey, ketchup, Worcestershire sauce, hot sauce, and 1 tablespoon of the Sweet Rib Rub. Mix well to combine and set in the refrigerator until ready to use.

2. Make the ribs. Using a paper towel, peel the membrane off of the backs of the rib racks and discard. Generously coat the ribs in a thin coat of mustard, and sprinkle all over with Sweet Rib Rub.

3. Supply your smoker with wood pellets and follow the start-up procedure. Preheat the grill, with the lid closed, to 275° F. If you're using a gas or charcoal grill set it up for low, indirect heat. Place the ribs meaty-side up and grill for 2-3 hours. Once the ribs have grilled for 2-3 hours, fill a spray bottle with 2 cups of apple juice and spray the ribs to keep them moist. Continue to grill the ribs, spraying every 45 minutes, until the meat bends slightly at the ends when lifted and is a deep mahogany color, about another 2-3 hours.

4. Remove the ribs from the grill and brush with mustard sauce, then slice and serve immediately.

Orange & Maple Baked Ham

Servings: 2

Cooking Time: 120 Minutes

Ingredients:

- 2/3 Cup orange juice
- 1/3 Cup maple syrup
- 1/3 Cup Marmalade, Orange
- 1/8 Cup Dijon mustard
- 1 1/3 Tablespoon apple cider vinegar
- 1/2 Teaspoon ground cinnamon
- 1/8 Teaspoon ground cloves
- 2/3 ham

Directions:

1. Supply your smoker with wood pellets and follow the start-up procedure. Preheat the grill, with the lid closed, to 325° F.

2. Meanwhile, make the glaze: In a small saucepan, combine the orange juice, the maple syrup, marmalade, mustard, vinegar, cinnamon, and cloves.

3. Warm over low heat, whisking to combine the ingredients. Remove from the heat and reserve.

4. Place ham in large roasting pan lined with aluminum foil. Place pan on grill and cook for 1.5 hours. Grill: 325 ˚F

5. Open grill and glaze ham with reserved mixture. Continue cooking for another 30 minutes or until a thermometer is inserted into the thickest part of the meat and reaches an internal temperatures of 135 degrees F. Grill: 325 ˚F Probe: 135 ˚F

6. Remove ham from grill and allow to rest for 20 minutes before serving.

7. Warm remaining sauce and serve with ham if desired. Enjoy!

Smoked Traeger Pulled Pork

Servings: 8

Cooking Time: 540 Minutes

Ingredients:

- 1 (6-9 lb) bone-in pork shoulder
- Pork & Poultry Rub
- 2 Cup apple cider
- 'Que BBQ Sauce

Directions:

1. Supply your smoker with wood pellets and follow the start-up procedure. Preheat the grill, with the lid closed, to 250° F.

2. While the Traeger comes to temperature, trim excess fat off pork butt.

3. Generously season with Traeger Pork & Poultry Rub on all sides and let sit for 20 minutes.

4. Place the pork butt fat side up directly on the grill grate and cook until the internal temperature reaches 160℉, about 3 to 5 hours. Grill: 250 ℉ Probe: 160 ℉

5. Remove the pork butt from the grill.

6. On a large baking sheet, stack 4 large pieces of aluminum foil on top of each other, ensuring they are wide enough to wrap the pork butt entirely on all sides. If not, overlap the foil pieces to create a wider base. Place the pork butt in the center on the foil, then bring up the sides of the foil a little bit before pouring the apple cider on top of the pork butt. Wrap the foil tightly around the pork, ensuring the cider does not escape.

7. Place the foil-wrapped pork butt back on the grill fat side up and cook until the internal temperature reaches 204℉, in the thickest part of the meat, about 3 to 4 hours longer depending on the size of the pork butt. Grill: 250 ℉ Probe: 204 ℉

8. Remove from the grill. Allow the pork to rest for 45 minutes in the foil packet.

9. Remove the pork from the foil and pour off any excess liquid into a fat separator.

10. Place the pork in a large dish and shred the meat, removing and discarding the bone and any excess fat. Add separated liquid back into pork and season to taste with additional Traeger Big Game Rub. Optionally, add Traeger 'Que BBQ Sauce or your favorite BBQ sauce to taste.

Sweet Smoked Country Ribs

Servings: 12-15

Cooking Time: 240 Minutes

Ingredients:

- 2 pounds country-style ribs
- 1 batch Sweet Brown Sugar Rub
- 2 tablespoons light brown sugar
- 1 cup Pepsi or other cola
- ¼ cup The Ultimate BBQ Sauce

Directions:

1. Supply your smoker with wood pellets and follow the start-up procedure. Preheat the grill, with the lid closed, to 180℉.

2. Sprinkle the ribs with the rub and use your hands to work the rub into the meat.

3. Place the ribs directly on the grill grate and smoke for 3 hours.

4. Remove the ribs from the grill and place them on enough aluminum foil to wrap them completely. Dust the brown sugar over the ribs.

5. Increase the grill's temperature to 300℉.

6. Fold in three sides of the foil around the ribs and add the cola. Fold in the last side, completely enclosing the ribs and liquid. Return the ribs to the grill and cook for 45 minutes.

7. Remove the ribs from the foil and place them on the grill grate. Baste all sides of the ribs with barbecue sauce. Cook for 15 minutes more to caramelize the sauce.

8. Remove the ribs from the grill and serve immediately.

Bbq Pulled Pork Hash

Servings: 4
Cooking Time: 30 Minutes

Ingredients:
*   1/2 Cup carrots, peeled and cut into 1 inch pieces
*   1/2 Cup beets
*   1/2 Cup small new potatoes
*   1/2 Cup asparagus
*   1 Tablespoon olive oil
*   leftover pulled pork
*   3 egg

Directions:

1. Supply your smoker with wood pellets and follow the start-up procedure. Preheat the grill, with the lid closed, to 375° F.

2. Chop all vegetables into even pieces, about 1/2 inch cubes. Pre heat a cast iron pan over Medium-High heat.

3. Add a Tablespoon of olive oil then the carrots, new potatoes, and beets. Season with salt and pepper to taste and sauté stirring every few minutes until vegetables are cooked through (about 8 to 10 minutes).

4. Add the asparagus and cook an additional 2 minutes. Add a layer of pulled pork over vegetables. Crack 3 eggs over that being careful not to break the yokes.

5. Place into preheated Traeger and cook for about 10 minutes or until eggs are just set.

Remove from grill and serve immediately with your favorite hot sauce. Enjoy! Grill: 375 °F

Bbq 3-2-1 St. Louis Ribs

Servings: 6
Cooking Time: 360 Minutes

Ingredients:
*   2 Rack St. Louis-style ribs
*   Pork & Poultry Rub
*   1/2 Cup brown sugar, divided
*   1/3 Cup honey, divided
*   1 Cup BBQ Sauce
*   BBQ Sauce

Directions:

1. If your butcher has not done so already, remove the thin silverskin membrane from the bone-side of the ribs by working the tip of a butter knife underneath the membrane over a middle bone. Use paper towels to get a firm grip, then tear the membrane off.

2. Season both sides of the ribs generously with Traeger Pork & Poultry Rub.

3. Supply your smoker with wood pellets and follow the start-up procedure. Preheat the grill, with the lid closed, to 180° F.

4. Smoke the ribs, meat-side up for 3 hours. Transfer the ribs to a rimmed baking sheet and increase the grill temperature to 225°F. Preheat the grill with the lid closed. Grill: 225 °F

5. Tear off four long sheets of heavy-duty aluminum foil. Top with a rack of ribs. Sprinkle half the brown sugar on the rack then top with half the honey. Tightly wrap the ribs with the foil to create a leak-proof pouch. Repeat with remaining rack of ribs. Grill: 225 °F

6. Return the foiled ribs to the grill, meat side down and cook for an additional two hours. Grill: 225 °F

7. Carefully remove the foil from the ribs – watch out for hot steam – and brush the ribs on both sides with your favorite Traeger BBQ sauce. Discard the foil. Arrange the ribs directly on the grill grate, bone side down and continue to grill until the sauce tightens, about 30 minutes to 60 minutes more. Let the ribs rest for a few minutes before serving. Enjoy! Grill: 225 °F

Jamaican Jerk Pork Chops

Servings: 4
Cooking Time: 720 Minutes

Ingredients:

- 4 thick pork rib or loin chops, each about 12oz (340g) and 1 inch (2.5cm) thick
- for the marinade
- ½ to 1 Scotch bonnet or habanero pepper, destemmed, deseeded, and coarsely chopped, plus more
- 2 scallions, trimmed, white and green parts coarsely chopped
- 1 garlic clove, peeled and coarsely chopped
- juice of 1 lime
- 2 tbsp vegetable oil
- 2 tbsp distilled water
- 1 tbsp light soy sauce
- 2 tsp coarsely chopped fresh thyme leaves
- 2 tsp peeled and minced fresh ginger
- 2 tsp dark brown sugar or low-carb substitute, plus more
- 1 tsp coarse salt, plus more
- ½ tsp freshly ground black pepper
- ½ tsp ground allspice
- ½ tsp ground nutmeg
- ½ tsp ground cinnamon

Directions:

1. In a blender, make the jerk marinade by combining the ingredients. Blend until fairly smooth. Taste for seasoning, adding more Scotch bonnet, brown sugar, or salt. Place the pork chops in a resealable plastic bag and pour the marinade over them, turning and massaging the bag to thoroughly coat the meat. Refrigerate for 2 to 4 hours.

2. Supply your smoker with wood pellets and follow the start-up procedure. Preheat the grill, with the lid closed, to 425° F.

3. Remove the pork from the marinade and scrape off the excess. (Discard the marinade.) Grill the chops until the internal temperature reaches 145°F (63°C), about 6 to 8 minutes per side.

4. Transfer the chops to a platter. Let rest for 2 minutes before serving.

Cider Glazed Baked Holiday Ham

Servings: 6
Cooking Time: 120 Minutes

Ingredients:

- 3 apples, cored and cut into thick slices
- 1 Large ham
- 4 Cup apple cider, divided
- 1/4 Cup bourbon
- 1/4 Cup Dijon mustard
- 1/4 Cup honey or maple syrup
- 1/2 Teaspoon ground cinnamon
- 1/4 Teaspoon ground cloves
- 1 Pinch ground nutmeg or allspice

Directions:

1. Supply your smoker with wood pellets and follow the start-up procedure. Preheat the grill, with the lid closed, to 325° F.

2. Line a roasting pan with heavy-duty foil for easier clean-up.

3. Arrange the apple slices in the bottom of the roasting pan for a natural roasting rack. Place ham on top of the apple slices and pour remaining 1 cup of apple cider around the ham.

4. Place roasting pan directly on grill grate and bake for 1-1/2 hours. Grill: 325 °F

5. For the glaze, combine remaining 3 cups of apple cider and bourbon in a small saucepan and bring to a boil over medium-high heat. Simmer until reduced by one-third. Whisk in the mustard, honey, cinnamon, cloves and nutmeg.

6. Glaze ham with apple cider mixture as needed (use any left over for serving) and continue cooking for another 30 minutes or until a thermometer inserted into the thickest part of the meat reaches an internal temperatures of 140°F. Grill: 325 °F Probe: 140 °F

7. Remove ham from grill and allow to rest for 20 minutes before serving.

8. Warm remaining sauce and serve with ham if desired. Enjoy!

Baked Eggs In Bacon Nest

Servings: 4
Cooking Time: 30 Minutes

Ingredients:
- 6 Strips bacon
- 6 Whole eggs
- 1/4 Teaspoon salt
- 1/4 Teaspoon pepper

Directions:

1. Supply your smoker with wood pellets and follow the start-up procedure. Preheat the grill, with the lid closed, to 375° F.

2. Place bacon strips directly on the grill grate and cook about 15 minutes. Transfer to a paper towel and pat dry.

3. Spray a muffin tin liberally with cooking spray. Line each muffin cup with one slice of bacon then crack one egg into each cup. Season each cup with salt and pepper.

4. Transfer muffin tin to the grill and cook for 15-20 minutes until the bacon is crisp, whites are just set, and yolk is still runny. Enjoy!

Spiced Grilled Pork Chops

Servings: 4
Cooking Time: 30 Minutes

Ingredients:
- 3 Tbsp Black Peppercorns, Ground
- 1 Tbsp Coriander, Seed
- 1/4 Cup Cumin
- 1 - 2 Tsp Dry Rub
- 1 Tsp Olive Oil
- 4 Pork, Chop Bone-In
- 1 1/2 Tsp Salt
- 2 Tbsp Sugar

Directions:

1. Supply your smoker with wood pellets and follow the start-up procedure. Preheat the grill, with the lid open, to 450° F.

2. Combine the cumin seeds, whole black peppercorns, and coriander seeds in a cast iron skillet. Stir over medium heat for about 8 minutes until toasted. Let them cool slightly. Finely grind toasted spices in a blender and transfer to a small bowl, then mix in sugar and salt.

3.   Rub the spices into the pork chops on both sides. Place cast iron skillet inside the grill. Once hot, add the olive oil to the skillet and coat the bottom. Sprinkle the pork chops with salt, and then add to the skillet. Make sure that each pork chop has enough space in between one another. Cook the chops for about 30 minutes. Once pork chops are fully cooked, turn off the grill, remove skillet, plate and enjoy!

Grilled Pork Tacos Al Pastor

Servings: 8
Cooking Time: 15 Minutes

Ingredients:

- 2 Tsp Annatto Powder
- Cilantro, Chopped
- Corn Tortillas
- 2 Tsp Cumin
- 1 Tsp Granulated Garlic
- 2 Tbsp Guajillo Chili Powder
- Jalapeno Pepper, Minced
- Lime, Wedges
- 1 Tsp Oregano, Dried
- 1/2 Tsp Pepper
- 1/2 Cup Pineapple, Juice
- 1/2 Pineapple, Skinned & Cored
- 2 Lbs Pork Shoulder, Boneless, Sliced Thin
- 1 1/2 Tsp Salt
- 2 Tbsp Tomato Paste
- 2 Tbsp Vegetable Oil
- 1/4 Cup White Vinegar
- Yellow Onion, Chopped

Directions:

1.   Prepare marinade: In a mixing bowl, whisk together pineapple juice, vinegar, oil, tomato paste, chili powder, annatto, cumin, granulated garlic, oregano, salt, and pepper. Set aside.

2.   Slice pork shoulder into thin slices (around ¼" thick), then place in a resealable plastic bag. Pour marinade over pork, seal bag, and turn to coat. Refrigerate overnight.

3.   Supply your smoker with wood pellets and follow the start-up procedure. Preheat the grill, with the lid open, to 450° F. If using a gas or charcoal grill, set it up for high heat.

4.   Remove the pork from the marinade and set on the grill. Grill over high heat for 3 to 5 minutes, turning frequently. Transfer to a cutting board to rest for 10 minutes, then slice thin.

5.   Grill pineapple for 3 minutes, turning once. Set aside on a cutting board, and chop once cooled.

6.   Assemble tacos: tortillas, pork, pineapple, jalapeño, onion, and cilantro. Serve warm with fresh lime wedges.

Spiced Pork Belly

Servings: 4
Cooking Time: 130 Minutes

Ingredients:

- 2lb (1kg) skinless pork belly
- for the rub
- 2 tbsp fine kosher salt
- 2 tbsp granulated white or light brown sugar or low-carb substitute
- 2 tsp freshly ground black pepper
- 2 tsp ground mustard
- 2 tsp Chinese five-spice powder

Directions:

1.   In a small bowl, make the rub by combining the ingredients. Mix well. Lightly season the pork belly on all sides with the rub. Cover and refrigerate overnight.

2. Supply your smoker with wood pellets and follow the start-up procedure. Preheat the grill, with the lid closed, to 450° F.

3. Place the pork belly on the grate and roast for 30 minutes, turning once. Lower the temperature to 275°F (135°C). Roast the pork until tender and the internal temperature reaches 185°F (85°C), about 1 to 1½ hours more.

4. Remove the pork belly from the grill and let cool completely. Wrap tightly in plastic wrap and refrigerate until firm and well chilled.

5. Preheat the grill to 450°F (232°C).

6. Cut the pork belly into slices, slabs, or cubes. Place the pork on the grate and grill until the edges crisp, about 8 to 10 minutes, turning as needed.

7. Remove the pork from the grill and serve immediately.

Championship Ribs With Kansas City Style

Servings: 4
Cooking Time: 210 Minutes

Ingredients:
- Apple Juice
- 2 Racks Baby Back Rib
- 2 Cups Brown Sugar
- 24 Oz Dijon Mustard
- 4 Tbsp Sweet Rib Rub
- Spray Bottle

Directions:

1. Pour Dijon Mustard into a mixing bowl. Mix in brown sugar until mustard taste diminishes and a sweet taste takes over.

2. Generally, you will use a half bag of brown sugar for 2 bottles and the whole bag for 4 bottles.

The key is for the tangy mustard taste to turn sweet.

3. When this mix is brushed on the ribs the mix of pork flavor and this glaze will produce a sweet and sassy result. The easiest way to mix is with an electric mixer but a whisk will do nicely. This will become very thick and sticky.

4. Supply your smoker with wood pellets and follow the start-up procedure. Preheat the grill, with the lid open, to 275° F.

5. Place ribs, back side down, on the cooking grid. Note: If you are doing multiple slabs, I suggest you use a rib rack. Most Rib Racks will hold 6 slabs. This will allow ribs to cook evenly. The rib rack allows for more slabs since ribs will sit in rack on their edge. Try to put meatier side up.

6. Spray ribs thoroughly with apple juice every 30-40 minutes. Apple Juice not only helps to keep meat moist and juicy while cooking, the acidity also helps to break down the muscles, thus tenderizing as well. I have had people tell me they prefer Pineapple juice or a mixture of apple and pineapple. Personally, I can't tell the difference, but you can experiment for yourself if you want to. The result will be same.

7. Note: How to tell when ribs are done? It is hard to measure temp of a rib with a meat thermometer due to the meat between the bones being so tight. You can get a false reading if the thermometer is touching a bone. Take your tongs and pick up slab in the middle. If the rib folds over and is limp and the meat just begins to pull away from the bone, they are done.

8. Remove ribs from grill and place in a pan (long enough for ribs to fit)

9. Glaze both sides of ribs with a light coat of the sassy glaze. This is a flavor enhancer, not a cover up. Just a light coat is plenty. If you really like the glaze there will generally always be some left over, and you can add to your desire while on the plate.

10. Wrap ribs in foil and let stand for 15 minutes

11. Serve (you can serve in slab form and let each guest cut his own or I like to cut ribs and serve as single bones.

12. Enjoy!

Whiskey- & Cider-brined Pork Shoulder

Servings: 8

Cooking Time: 540 Minutes

Ingredients:

- 1 bone-in pork shoulder, about 5 to 7lb (2.3 to 3.2kg)
- fresh coarsely ground black pepper
- granulated garlic
- 1 cup apple juice or apple cider
- low-carb barbecue sauce, warmed
- hamburger buns (optional)
- for the brine
- 1 gallon (3.8 liters) cold distilled water
- 1 cup coarse salt
- 1¼ cup whiskey, divided
- ½ cup light brown sugar or low-carb substitute

Directions:

1. In a large saucepot on the stovetop over medium-high heat, make the brine by bringing the water, salt, 1 cup of whiskey, and brown sugar to a boil. Stir with a long-handled wooden spoon until the salt and sugar dissolve. Let the brine cool to room temperature. Cover and cool completely in the refrigerator.

2. Submerge the pork in the brine. If it floats, place a resealable bag of ice on top. Refrigerate for 24 hours.

3. Supply your smoker with wood pellets and follow the start-up procedure. Preheat the grill, with the lid closed, to 250° F.

4. Remove the pork shoulder from the brine and pat dry with paper towels. (Discard the brine.) Season the pork with pepper and granulated garlic. Place the pork on the grate and smoke until the internal temperature reaches 165°F (74°C), about 5 hours.

5. Transfer the pork to an aluminum foil roasting pan and add the apple juice and the remaining ¼ cup of whiskey. Cover tightly with aluminum foil. Place the pan on the grate and cook the pork until the bone releases easily from the meat and the internal temperature reaches 200°F (93°C), about 3 hours more. (Be careful when lifting a corner of the foil to check on the roast because steam will escape.)

6. Remove the pan from the grill and let the pork rest for 20 minutes. Reserve the juices.

7. Wearing heatproof gloves, pull the pork into chunks. Discard the bone or any large lumps of fat. Pull the meat into shreds and transfer to a clean aluminum foil roasting pan. Moisten with the barbecue sauce or serve the sauce on the side. Stir in some of the drippings—not too much because you don't want the pork to be swimming in its juices. Serve on buns (if using).

Baked Bacon Caramel Popcorn

Servings: 6
Cooking Time: 30 Minutes

Ingredients:

- 1 Pound bacon
- 1 Cup popcorn kernels
- 2 Stick unsalted butter
- 1/2 Teaspoon salt
- 2 Cup brown sugar, packed
- 1/4 Cup Kentucky bourbon
- 11 Teaspoon baking soda
- 2 Teaspoon vanilla

Directions:

1. Supply your smoker with wood pellets and follow the start-up procedure. Preheat the grill, with the lid closed, to 350° F.

2. Lay bacon strips directly on the grill grate and cook for 15 to 20 minutes or until fat is rendered and bacon is lightly browned. Remove from grill and chop into 1/2 inch pieces. Set aside. Grill: 350 °F

3. While grill is cooling, pop kernels in a popcorn maker. Place popped kernels and bacon in a large bowl and set aside.

4. In a medium saucepan over medium-high heat, combine butter, salt and sugar. Bring the mixture to a boil and cook until an instant-read thermometer reads 275°F. Immediately remove from heat and whisk in bourbon, vanilla and baking powder. Use caution because it will bubble up and release steam.

5. Reduce grill temperature to 225°F and let cool for 10 to 15 minutes. Grill: 225 °F

6. Pour caramel sauce over bacon and popcorn and toss to coat. Spread popcorn out onto a large sheet tray lined with a piece of parchment paper.

7. Place sheet tray directly on the grill grate and cook at 225°F for 15 to 20 minutes, watching closely to make sure the caramel doesn't burn. Grill: 225 °F

8. Remove from grill and pour popcorn on a counter lined with parchment paper. Let cool 30 minutes or until caramel has set. Enjoy!

Smoked Pork Tomato Tamales

Servings: 6-8
Cooking Time: 60 Minutes

Ingredients:

- 1 Boneless, Netted Pork Roast
- 1 Cup, Fresh Cilantro, Chopped
- 3 Cloves Garlic, Peeled
- 20 Dried Cornhusks
- 1 Tbsp Lime Juice
- ¼ Cup Olive Oil
- 1 Onion, Quartered
- 4 - 6 Cups Prepared Masa Harina Tamale Dough
- 3 – 4 Serrano Peppers, Deseeded
- 1 Tbsp Sweet Heat Rub
- 1 Lb. Tomatillos, Husked And Washed

Directions:

1. Began by soaking the corn husks in a pan filled with water. Soak for 2 – 4 hours, or if needed, overnight.

2. Unwrap the tomatillos from their shell and place all of them into a grill basket followed by a few Serranos, deseeded, garlic cloves and 1 onion cut into quarters.

3. Supply your smoker with wood pellets and follow the start-up procedure. Preheat the grill, with the lid open, to 400° F. If you're using a gas or charcoal grill, set it up for medium low heat, and use smoke chips to fill your grill with smoke

for 15 minutes. Place the grill basket filled with your vegetables and roast them over an open flame on your smoker until vegetables have become charred.

4. Place tomatillos, peppers, garlic and onions in a bowl, cover with plastic wrap, and let stand until cool enough to handle, 10 to 15 minutes.

5. Season the pork roast generously with Sweet Heat Rub and grill at 350°F for 1 hour until the roast has a nice crust on the outside.

6. While the pork roast is cooking, add a handful of cilantro, charred vegetables, 1 tbsp of Sweet Heat Rub, 1 tbsp lime juice, and ¼ cup of olive oil to a food processor. Pulse in food processor until mixture is consistent. Set aside

7. After the pork roast has been grilled for an hour, turn heat down to 275°F. Put roast in pan with about a cup of water, cover with aluminum foil and cook for another 4 hours or until the roast can be shredded. Pour chile verde sauce over shredded pork and toss to combine.

8. To being assembling tamales, place a corn husk on a work surface. Place 2-3 tablespoons of tamale dough on larger end of husk and spread into a rectangle, about ¼" thick, leaving a small border along the edge. Place large tablespoon of chili and pork filling on top of dough. Fold over sides of husk so dough surrounds filling, then fold bottom of husk up and secure closed by tying a thin strip of husk around tamale.

9. To cook tamales, place them in a large metal colander over a large stockpot filled with water. Cover and let steam for 1 hour. After the tamales have been steamed, take them off and grill them at 350°F for about 10-20 minutes until corn husks have charred marks.

The Dan Patrick Show Baked Chili Cheese Dog Cups

Servings: 6
Cooking Time: 30 Minutes

Ingredients:
- 2 Cup Chili With Beans, Your Choice
- 2 Olympia Provisions Franks
- 1 Can Pillsbury Grands Buttermilk Biscuits

Directions:
1. Supply your smoker with wood pellets and follow the start-up procedure. Preheat the grill, with the lid closed, to 350° F.

2. Combine chili and sliced hot dogs in a medium bowl. Open biscuits and separate into 8 biscuits.

3. Place each biscuit in a lightly greased muffin tin and press down on the sides and bottom to create a cup. Spoon a little bit of the chili hot dog mixture into each cup.

4. Place muffin tin directly on the grill grate and cook 30 minutes until biscuits are golden brown and chili is warmed. Grill: 350 °F

5. Let chili cups cool for five minutes before unmolding. Finish with your choice of toppings. Enjoy!

Traeger Pulled Pork Sandwiches

Servings: 8
Cooking Time: 660 Minutes

Ingredients:
- 1 (5-7 lb) bone-in pork shoulder
- Pork & Poultry Rub
- 2 Cup apple juice, in food-grade spray bottle
- BBQ Sauce
- 10 hamburger buns
- coleslaw, for serving

Directions:

1. Generously season pork roast on all sides with Traeger Pork & Poultry rub.

2. Supply your smoker with wood pellets and follow the start-up procedure. Preheat the grill, with the lid closed, to 225° F.

3. Put the roast on the grill grate, fat-side up and smoke for 3 hours. Spray the roast with apple juice every hour after the first hour. Grill: 225 ˚F

4. After 3 hours, transfer pork to a disposable aluminum foil pan large enough to hold the roast. Increase the grill temperature to 250°F, and continue to cook for 6 to 8 additional hours, or until an instant-read meat thermometer inserted in the thickest part, but not touching bone, registers 203°F. If the pork starts to brown too much, cover it loosely with aluminum foil. Grill: 250 ˚F Probe: 203 ˚F

5. Carefully transfer the pork roast to a cutting board and let it rest for 20 minutes. Pour the juices from the bottom of the pan into a gravy separator. Discard any fat that has floated to the top.

6. With your hands (preferably protected from the heat with lined, heavy-duty rubber gloves) pull the pork into chunks. Discard the bone and any lumps of fat, including the cap. Pull each chunk into shreds and transfer to a large mixing bowl.

7. Season with additional rub and moisten with the reserved pork juice. Add your favorite Traeger BBQ sauce to the pulled pork and mix well.

8. Pile the pork mixture on the hamburger buns and serve with coleslaw. Enjoy!

Beer Pork Belly Chili Con Carne

Servings: 4

Cooking Time: 120 Minutes

Ingredients:

- Avocado, Diced
- 2 Bay Leaves
- 1 Lbs Beef Stew Meat
- 12 Oz Beef Stock
- 12 Oz Beer, Bottle
- 15 Oz Black Beans, Rinsed And Drained
- 3 Tbsp Chili Powder
- Cilantro, Chopped
- 1 Tsp Coriander, Ground
- 2 Tsp Cumin, Ground
- 1 Tbsp Flour
- 4 Garlic Cloves, Minced
- 2 Tsp Mexican Oregano, Dried
- 2 Tbsp Olive Oil
- 2 Oz Pancetta, Diced
- Pork Belly, Cut Into 1 Inch Chunks
- 2 Red Onion, Chopped
- Rice, Cooked
- To Taste, Salt & Pepper
- Scallion, Sliced Thin
- 1/4 Cup Tomato Purée

Directions:

1. Supply your smoker with wood pellets and follow the start-up procedure. Preheat the grill, with the lid open, to 425° F. If using a gas or charcoal grill, set it up for medium-high heat. Place Dutch oven on grill and allow to preheat.

2. Heat the olive oil in the Dutch oven, then sauté the pancetta until crisp. Add the onions and sauté for 3 minutes, then add the garlic and sauté 1 minute, until fragrant. Remove mixture with a slotted spoon and set aside.

3. Add the pork belly and beef to the pot to brown, then add the chili powder, cumin,

oregano, and coriander. Add the flour and cook for 2 minutes, stirring constantly.

4. Add the beer, beef stock, and tomato purée. Stir well, then return the pancetta mixture to the pot. Add the black beans and bay leaves, then season with salt and pepper.

5. Bring chili to a simmer, then reduce temperature to 325°F and simmer, uncovered, for 2 hours, stirring occasionally, until meat is tender, and sauce has thickened.

6. Remove the chili from the grill, then serve warm with cooked rice, avocado, fresh cilantro, and scallions.

Smoky Bratwurst

Servings: 8 – 12
Cooking Time: 120 Minutes

Ingredients:
- 12 Fresh Bratwurst, Linked

Directions:

1. Supply your smoker with wood pellets and follow the start-up procedure. Preheat the grill, with the lid open, to 225° F. If using gas or charcoal grill, set it up for low indirect heat.

2. Place metal hooks on shelves about 6" apart. Cut bratwurst links into pairs and string on metal hooks. If you don't have metal hooks, you can place bratwurst directly on grill grate, but we recommend brushing the casing lightly in oil to ensure it doesn't stick during smoking.

3. Smoke bratwurst for one hour, then increase temperature to 300°F. Cook for one additional hour, or until bratwurst skin is golden brown and they've wrinkled slightly. If using a temperature probe, the brats are finished when internal temp reaches 160°F.

4. Remove from smoker and serve immediately. We recommend with buns and/or caramelized onions and sauerkraut.

Grilled Sugar Snap Peas And Smoked Bacon

Servings: 4
Cooking Time: 20 Minutes

Ingredients:
- 2 Pound Sugar Snap Peas, ends trimmed
- 2 Tablespoon extra-virgin olive oil
- 1 To Taste salt and pepper
- 1 Pound bacon
- 2 Tablespoon butter
- 2 Medium shallot, thinly sliced
- 1 Clove garlic, minced
- 1/4 Cup bourbon
- 2 Tablespoon maple syrup

Directions:

1. Supply your smoker with wood pellets and follow the start-up procedure. Preheat the grill, with the lid closed, to 350° F.

2. In a medium bowl, toss peas with olive oil and season with salt and pepper to taste.

3. Place a grill mat or tray on the grill grate to prevent peas from falling through the grates.

4. Place peas on grill mat and cook for 10 minutes until lightly browned and tender but still bright green. Grill: 350 °F

5. Place bacon slices on the grill next to peas and cook for 15-20 minutes or until fat is rendered and slightly crisp. Grill: 350 °F

6. While the bacon and peas cook, heat butter in a pan over medium-high heat.

7. Add shallot and garlic and sauté until tender and cooked through. Deglaze with bourbon and

cook until reduced by half. Add maple syrup and salt and pepper to taste. Set aside.

8. Remove bacon from grill and chop into 1/2-inch pieces.

9. Toss the bacon pieces with the grilled sugar snap peas and maple bourbon mixture. Enjoy!

Beer Braised Pork Belly And Beef

Servings: 4
Cooking Time: 90 Minutes

Ingredients:
- 1, Dark Beer, Any Brand
- 3 Cups Broth, Beef
- 1 Tablespoon Chinese Cooking Wine (Such As Shaoxing) Or Dry Sherry Wine
- 1 Teaspoon Chinese Five Spice Powder
- 2, Smashed Garlic, Cloves
- 1 Inch Knob Ginger, Peeled And Thinly Sliced
- 1 Onion, Sliced
- 2 Pounds Pork Belly, Cut Into 1 Inch Chunks
- 2 Tablespoons Rice Wine Vinegar
- 2 Tablespoons, Dark Soy Sauce, Low Sodium
- 3 Tablespoons Sugar

Directions:
1. Place a heavy dutch oven on a stovetop over medium high heat. Add the pork belly and brown on all sides, about 5 minutes. Once the pork belly has browned, add in the onion, ginger, and garlic, and stir well.

2. Pour the beer, beef broth, soy sauce, dark soy sauce, sugar, Chinese cooking wine, rice wine vinegar, and Chinese five spice powder into the pan. Place a lid on the pan and bring it to a boil. Once it boils, remove it from the heat.

3. Supply your smoker with wood pellets and follow the start-up procedure. Preheat the grill, with the lid open, to 325° F. Place the pan of pork belly on the grill and braise for 1 ½ hours, or until the pork belly is falling apart tender and glazed.

4. Remove the pork belly from the grill and serve immediately.

BAKING RECIPES

Smoked Lemon Tea

Servings: 6 - 8
Cooking Time: 60 Minutes

Ingredients:

- 8 Black Tea Bags
- 4 Cups Boiling Water
- 2 Cups Ice
- 8 Lemons
- 2 Cups Sugar
- 2 Cups Water

Directions:

1. Place the tea bags in a heat-safe pitcher. Bring 4 Cups of water to a boil and pour over tea bags. Let steep for 5-10 minutes. Remove tea bags and set pitcher aside to cool.

2. Turn on your grill and set to smoke mode. Combine 2 cups of sugar and 2 cups water in a small aluminum pan. Smoke for about 45 minutes, stirring occasionally, or until the mixture reduces to a thick, simple syrup. Remove from the grill and let it cool.

3. Supply your smoker with wood pellets and follow the start-up procedure. Preheat the grill, with the lid closed, to 450° F. If using a charcoal or gas grill, set heat to high.

4. Cut the lemons in half and sear over the flame broiler until charred, about 7 minutes. Remove from grill and set aside to cool.

5. Juice the lemons into a medium bowl. Pour lemon juice through a metal strainer into the tea pitcher to remove seeds and pulp.

6. Pour the cooled simple syrup into pitcher and stir until fully incorporated with tea and lemons. Add 2 cups of ice and refrigerate until serving.

Rosemary Cranberry Apple Sage Stuffing

Servings: 7
Cooking Time: 45 Minutes

Ingredients:

- 10 Cups Day Old Diced Bread, Sliced Loaf
- 2 1/2 Cups Broth, Chicken
- 1 Cup Butter, Unsalted
- 1 Cup Diced Celery, Cut
- 1 1/2 Cups Fresh Cranberries
- 1 Beaten Egg
- 1 Medium Granny Smith Apple, Peel, Core And Dice
- 2 Tbsp Minced Parsley, Fresh
- 1 Tbsp Minced Rosemary, Fresh
- 2 Tbsp Roughly Chopped Sage
- Salt And Pepper
- 1 Tbsp Minced Thyme
- 2 Cups Diced Yellow Onion, Sliced

Directions:

1. Supply your smoker with wood pellets and follow the start-up procedure. Preheat the grill, with the lid closed, to 350° F.

2. Melt butter over medium heat. Add onions then celery and cook until onions start to become translucent.

3. In a large bowl, mix together bread, apples, cranberries, cooked onion and celery mixture, and fresh herbs.

4. Add half of the chicken broth to the mixture and stir.

5. Beat together eggs and the rest of the chicken broth in a small bowl. Pour into the bread mixture and stir until completely combined.

6. Add salt and pepper to taste.

7. Pour stuffing into a cast iron pan or baking dish. Cover with foil and bake on the grill for 30 minutes. Remove the foil and cook for an additional 15 minutes.

8. Serve immediately and enjoy!

Baked Cheesy Parmesan Grits

Servings: 4

Cooking Time: 60 Minutes

Ingredients:
- 4 Cup chicken stock
- 3 Tablespoon butter
- 3/4 Teaspoon salt
- 1 Cup quick grits
- 1 Cup shredded cheddar cheese
- pepper
- 1/2 Cup Monterey Jack cheese, shredded
- 1/2 Cup whole milk
- 2 Large eggs

Directions:

1. Supply your smoker with wood pellets and follow the start-up procedure. Preheat the grill, with the lid closed, to 350° F.

2. Butter an 8" baking dish or a 10" cast iron pan.

3. Bring the chicken stock, butter, and salt to boil in medium saucepan. Gradually whisk in grits.

4. Reduce heat to medium and cook until mixture thickens slightly, stirring often about 8 minutes. Remove from heat.

5. Add cheeses and stir until melted. Season with pepper and salt to taste.

6. Whisk together milk and eggs in small bowl. Gradually whisk mixture into grits.

7. Pour the cheese grits into the buttered cast iron pan. Bake until grits feel firm to touch, about 1 hour. Grill: 350 °F

8. Remove from grill and let stand 10 minutes before serving. Enjoy!

Anzac Coconut Biscuits

Servings: 4

Cooking Time: 30 Minutes

Ingredients:
- This recipe makes a dozen biscuits.
- 1 cup rolled oats
- 3/4 cup raw sugar
- 3/4 cup desiccated coconut
- 1 cup plain flour, sifted
- 125 g butter, melted
- 2 tablespoons Golden Syrup
- 1/2 tsp bicarb soda
- 3 tablespoons boiling water

Directions:

1. Combine and mix thoroughly sifted flour, oats, sugar and coconut in a large bowl.

2. Melt the butter and Golden Syrup over low heat.

3. Add boiling water to the bicarb soda, once dissolved add into the butter/syrup mix, it will bubble/fizz up a bit.

4. Add the liquid into the dry ingredients and mix throughly.

5. Rolls the mix into golf ball size balls and layout on grease proof paper on baking tray and flatten the tops just slightly.

6. Space the balls with about 3 fingers between each ball as they will flatten to about triple the diameter as they cook.

7. Supply your smoker with wood pellets and follow the start-up procedure. Preheat the grill, with the lid closed, to 350° F. Cook for 25-30 minutes until golden brown.

8. Rest on cooling rack until at room temperature then store in air-tight container.

Basil Margherita Pizza

Servings: 6
Cooking Time: 25 Minutes

Ingredients:
- Basil, Chopped
- 2 Cups Flour, All-Purpose
- Mozzarella Cheese, Sliced Rounds
- 1 Cup Pizza Sauce
- 1 Teaspoon Salt
- 1 Teaspoon Sugar
- 1 Tomato, Sliced
- 1 Cup Water, Warm
- 1 Teaspoon Yeast, Instant

Directions:
1. Combine the water, yeast, and sugar in a small bowl and let sit for about 5 minutes.

2. In a large bowl, stir together the flour and salt. Pour in the yeast mixture and mix until a soft dough forms. Knead for about 2 minutes. Place in an oiled bowl and cover with a cloth. Let the dough sit and rise for about 45 minutes or until the dough has doubled in size.

3. Roll out on a flat, floured surface (or on a pizza stone) until you"ve reached your desired shape and thickness.

4. Supply your smoker with wood pellets and follow the start-up procedure. Preheat the grill, with the lid closed, to 350° F.

5. On the rolled out dough, pour on the pizza sauce, cheese, and then tomatoes and basil. Place in your Grill and bake for about 25 minutes, or until the cheese is melted and slightly golden brown.

Carrot Cake

Servings: 4-6
Cooking Time: 60 Minutes

Ingredients:
- 8 carrots, peeled and grated
- 4 eggs, at room temperature
- 1 cup vegetable oil
- ½ cup milk
- 1 teaspoon vanilla extract
- 2 cups sugar
- 2 cups self-rising or cake flour
- 2 teaspoons baking soda
- 1 teaspoon salt
- 1 cup finely chopped pecans
- Nonstick cooking spray or butter, for greasing
- 8 ounces cream cheese
- 1 cup confectioners' sugar
- 8 tablespoons (1 stick) unsalted butter, at room temperature
- 1 teaspoon vanilla extract
- ½ teaspoon salt
- 2 tablespoons to ¼ cup milk

Directions:
1. For the cake:

2. Supply your smoker with wood pellets and follow the start-up procedure. Preheat, with the lid closed, to 350°F.

3. In a food processor or blender, combine the grated carrots, eggs, oil, milk, and vanilla, and process until the carrots are finely minced.

4. In a large mixing bowl, combine the sugar, flour, baking soda, and salt.

5. Add the carrot mixture to the flour mixture and stir until well incorporated. Fold in the chopped pecans.

6. Coat a 9-by-13-inch baking pan with cooking spray.

7. Pour the batter into prepared pan and place on the grill grate. Close the lid and smoke for about 1 hour, or until a toothpick inserted in the center comes out clean.

8. Remove the cake from the grill and let cool completely.

9. For the frosting:

10. Using an electric mixer on low speed, beat the cream cheese, confectioners' sugar, butter, vanilla, and salt, adding 2 tablespoons to ¼ cup of milk to thin the frosting as needed.

11. Frost the cooled cake and slice to serve.

Baked Potatoes & Celery Root Au Gratin

Servings: 2
Cooking Time: 60 Minutes

Ingredients:

- 5 Tablespoon butter, softened
- 2 Large leeks, white parts only, cleaned and sliced into half moons
- kosher salt
- freshly ground black pepper
- 5 Small Yukon Gold potatoes, sliced 1/4 inch thick
- 2 Whole celery root, peeled and sliced 1/4 inch thick
- 2 Cup cream
- 1 Tablespoon minced sage
- 1 Cup shredded Gruyere or other hearty Swiss cheese, divided

Directions:

1. Supply your smoker with wood pellets and follow the start-up procedure. Preheat the grill, with the lid closed, to 400° F.

2. Butter a 9x13 baking dish with 1 tablespoon of the softened butter. In a medium frying pan over medium heat, melt the remaining butter. Add the leeks and a generous pinch of salt and pepper and cook, stirring often until softened, about 5 minutes.

3. Remove from the heat and allow to cool. Place the potato and celery root slices into a large mixing bowl. Add the cream, leek mixture, minced sage, 1 teaspoon salt, 1/2 teaspoon pepper and 1 cup cheese. Stir gently to coat.

4. Arrange a layer of potato and celery root slices so they're slightly overlapping in the prepared baking dish. Repeat two more times so there are three layers of potatoes. Pour remaining cream from the bowl over the gratin, then sprinkle the top with the remaining cup of cheese.

5. Cover the dish loosely with foil and bake on the grill for 45 minutes. Remove the foil and continue baking until the top is golden and bubbly and the potatoes are tender when pierced, about 30 to 45 minutes longer. Let stand for 10 minutes before serving. Enjoy!

Caramelized Bourbon Baked Pears

Servings: 4
Cooking Time: 30 Minutes

Ingredients:

- 3 Whole Pears, fresh
- 1/4 Cup brown sugar
- 1/4 Cup bourbon
- 2 Tablespoon butter, melted
- 1 Teaspoon vanilla extract

- 1/2 Teaspoon salt

Directions:

1. Supply your smoker with wood pellets and follow the start-up procedure. Preheat the grill, with the lid closed, to 325° F.

2. Peel and core the pears. Arrange them in a buttered baking dish.

3. In a small bowl, combine the brown sugar, bourbon, butter, vanilla, cinnamon and salt. Pour the bourbon mixture over the pears.

4. Place the baking dish on the grill grate, close the lid and bake for 30-35 minutes or until the pears are fork tender. Grill: 325 °F

5. Transfer to a serving plate and spoon the caramelized bourbon mixture over the pears.

6. Serve warm over vanilla ice cream. Enjoy!

Blueberry Sour Cream Muffins

Servings: 8
Cooking Time: 25 Minutes

Ingredients:

- 2 Cup flour
- 1/2 Teaspoon salt
- 1/2 Teaspoon baking soda
- 1/2 Cup butter
- 3/4 Cup sugar, plus more for muffin tops
- 2 Large eggs
- 3/4 Cup sour cream
- 1 1/2 Teaspoon vanilla extract
- 1 1/2 Cup blueberries, fresh or thawed

Directions:

1. In a small mixing bowl, whisk together the flour, salt and baking soda.

2. In another bowl, using a wooden spoon or a mixer, beat the butter and sugar until light-colored and fluffy. Beat in the eggs, one at a time. Stir in sour cream and vanilla.

3. Add the flour mixture gradually and mix just until incorporated. Using a rubber spatula, gently fold in the blueberries.

4. Line a 12-cup muffin tin with the cupcake liners. Using an ice cream scoop or spoon, fill each muffin cup two-thirds full with the batter. Sprinkle sugar evenly over the top of each muffin.

5. Supply your smoker with wood pellets and follow the start-up procedure. Preheat the grill, with the lid closed, to 375° F.

6. Bake the muffins 25 to 30 minutes, or until a toothpick inserted comes out clean. Served warm and with butter. Grill: 375 °F

Baked Molten Chocolate Cake

Servings: 4
Cooking Time: 20 Minutes

Ingredients:

- all-purpose flour
- butter
- 4 Ounce butter
- 6 Ounce Chocolate, Bittersweet
- 2 eggs
- 2 egg yolk
- 1/2 Cup sugar
- 1 Pinch salt

Directions:

1. Supply your smoker with wood pellets and follow the start-up procedure. Preheat the grill, with the lid closed, to 450° F.

2. Butter and flour four (6oz) ramekins. Tap out excess flour. Place ramekins on a baking sheet and reserve.

3. Melt butter and chocolate in a double boiler over simmering water. In a medium bowl, beat eggs and yolks with sugar and salt on high until thick and pale.

4. Whisk in chocolate until smooth and quickly fold into the egg mixture along with flour.

5. Spoon the batter into prepared ramekins and bake for 20 minutes or until sides are firm but centers are soft. Grill: 450 ˚F

6. Let cool for 1 minute, then cover each with an inverted dessert plate. Carefully turn each over, let stand 10 seconds, then unmold.

7. Serve immediately with Maple Ice Cream with Candied Bacon. Enjoy!

Bacon Chocolate Chip Cookies

Servings: 2
Cooking Time: 10-12 Minutes

Ingredients:

- 2¾ cups all-purpose flour
- 1½ teaspoons baking soda
- ½ teaspoon salt
- 12 tablespoons (1½ sticks) unsalted butter, softened
- 1 cup light brown sugar
- 1 cup granulated sugar
- 2 eggs, at room temperature
- 2½ teaspoons apple cider vinegar
- 1 teaspoon vanilla extract
- 2 cups semisweet chocolate chips
- 8 slices bacon, cooked and crumbled

Directions:

1. In a large bowl, combine the flour, baking soda, and salt, and mix well.

2. In a separate large bowl, using an electric mixer on medium speed, cream the butter and sugars. Reduce the speed to low and mix in the eggs, vinegar, and vanilla.

3. With the mixer speed still on low, slowly incorporate the dry ingredients, chocolate chips, and bacon pieces.

4. Supply your smoker with wood pellets and follow the start-up procedure. Preheat, with the lid closed, to 375˚F.

5. Line a large baking sheet with parchment paper.

6. Drop rounded teaspoonfuls of cookie batter onto the prepared baking sheet and place on the grill grate. Close the lid and smoke for 10 to 12 minutes, or until the cookies are browned around the edges.

Skillet Buttermilk Cornbread

Servings: 6
Cooking Time: 25 Minutes

Ingredients:

- 1 Cup Cornmeal
- 1 Cup all-purpose flour
- 1/3 Cup granulated sugar
- 1 Teaspoon salt
- 1 Teaspoon baking powder
- 1 1/2 Cup buttermilk
- 2 Whole eggs
- 8 Tablespoon butter, melted

Directions:

1. Grease a cast iron skillet or 9-inch square baking pan with bacon fat. Put a 10-inch well-seasoned cast iron skillet on the grill grate. If using a regular baking pan, do not preheat.

2. Supply your smoker with wood pellets and follow the start-up procedure. Preheat the grill, with the lid closed, to 400˚ F.

3. In a large mixing bowl, combine the cornmeal, flour, sugar, salt, and baking powder and whisk to mix thoroughly. Make a well in the center of the dry ingredients.

4. In a separate mixing bowl, whisk together the buttermilk and eggs until well-combined. Add

the melted butter. Pour into the dry ingredients and mix until the batter is fairly smooth. Do not overmix.

5. Carefully pour the batter into the preheated skillet. Bake for 20 to 25 minutes, or until the top is firm and a tester inserted in the center of the cornbread comes out clean. Be careful when removing the skillet from the grill as it will be very hot. Let the cornbread cool slightly on a trivet or cooling rack before slicing into wedges or squares.

Chicken Pot Pie

Servings: 6
Cooking Time: 60 Minutes

Ingredients:
- 2 Chicken, Boneless/Skinless
- 1 Cream Of Chicken Soup, Can
- 1 Tsp Curry Powder
- 1/2 Cup Mayo
- 1 1/2 Cups Mixed Frozen Vegetables
- 1 Onion, Sliced
- 2 Frozen Pie Shell, Deep
- 1/2 Cup Sour Cream

Directions:
1. Supply your smoker with wood pellets and follow the start-up procedure. Preheat the grill, with the lid closed, to 425° F.
2. Cut the onion in half and place on the grates of the grill. If you"re using fresh chicken breasts, barbecue the chicken at the same time as the onions. The chicken is fully cooked when the internal temperature reached 170F. While the onion and chicken are cooking, prepare the pie crust by putting one crust in a pie plate. When the chicken and onions are done, shred chicken and chop onion into small pieces and place in the

prepared pie plate along with the mixed vegetables.

3. Combine cream of chicken soup, mayo, sour cream, and curry powder in a bowl. Pour into the pie crust with the chicken and mix to combine. Wet the sides of the bottom crust with a small amount of water and top with the second pie crust. Push gently along the sides of the crust to seal the two pie crusts together.

4. Place in the and bake for 40 minutes, or until the crust is golden brown. Serve hot.

Delicious Peanut Butter Cookies

Servings: 24
Cooking Time: 15 Minutes

Ingredients:
- 1 Egg
- 1 Cup Peanut Butter
- 1 Cup Sugar

Directions:
1. Supply your smoker with wood pellets and follow the start-up procedure. Preheat the grill, with the lid closed, to High heat.
2. Combine all ingredients in a bowl. Drop tablespoon amounts of dough on a prepared baking sheet and bake in your Grill for 15-20 minutes. Allow cookies to cool for 5 minutes on the baking sheet before you enjoy!

Smoky Pimento Cheese Cornbread

Servings: 4
Cooking Time: 30 Minutes

Ingredients:
- 2 Tsp Baking Powder
- 2 Cups Buttermilk, Low Fat

- 1/2 Cup Cornmeal, Yellow
- 2 Egg
- 1 1/2 Cups Flour, All-Purpose
- 16 Oz Pimento Cheese Spread
- 2 Tbsp Bacon Cheddar Seasoning
- 1/4 Cup Sugar

Directions:

1. Supply your smoker with wood pellets and follow the start-up procedure. Preheat the grill, with the lid closed, to 350° F. Place a cast iron skillet in the grill to preheat.

2. In a bowl, mix together the eggs, buttermilk, Bacon Cheddar Seasoning, and pimento cheese spread. Add in the sugar, baking powder, cornmeal and flour. Mix until well combined.

3. With cooking gloves, carefully remove the cast iron skillet from the grill, grease it, and add the cornbread batter.

4. Grill for 25-30 minutes, or until the cornbread is golden and pulling away from the edges of the skillet.

Baked Bourbon Maple Pumpkin Pie

Servings: 6-8
Cooking Time: 60 Minutes

Ingredients:

- 1/4 Cup Cocoa Powder, Unsweetened
- 1 Tablespoon Cocoa Powder, Unsweetened
- 3 1/2 Tablespoon sugar
- 1 Teaspoon salt
- 1 1/4 Cup all-purpose flour
- 1 Tablespoon all-purpose flour
- 6 Tablespoon butter
- 2 Tablespoon vegetable oil
- 1 Large Egg Yolk
- 1/2 Teaspoon apple cider vinegar
- 1/4 Cup ice water
- 1 Large egg, beaten
- 15 Ounce Pumpkin, canned
- 1/4 Cup sour cream
- 2 Tablespoon bourbon
- 1 Teaspoon ground cinnamon
- 1/2 Teaspoon salt
- 1/4 Teaspoon ground ginger
- 1/4 Teaspoon ground nutmeg
- 1/8 Teaspoon Allspice, ground
- 1/8 Teaspoon Mace, ground
- 3 Large eggs
- 3/4 Cup maple syrup
- 2 Tablespoon sugar
- 1/2 Vanilla Bean, halved
- 1 Cup heavy cream

Directions:

1. For the Chocolate Pie Dough: Pulse cocoa powder, granulated sugar, salt, and 1-1/4 cups plus 1 Tbsp flour in a food processor to combine. Add butter and shortening and pulse until mixture resembles coarse meal with a few pea-sized pieces of butter remaining. Transfer to a large bowl.

2. Whisk together the egg yolk, vinegar, and 1/4 cup ice water in a small bowl. Drizzle half of the egg mixture over flour mixture and, using a fork, mix gently just until combined. Add remaining egg mixture and mix until the dough just comes together (you will have some unincorporated pieces).

3. Turn out dough onto a lightly floured surface, flatten slightly, and cut into quarters. Stack pieces on top of one another. Placing unincorporated dry pieces of dough between layers, and press down to combine. Repeat process twice more (all pieces of dough should be incorporated at this

point). Form dough into a 1" thick disk. Wrap in plastic; chill at least 1 hour.

4. Roll out a disk of dough on a lightly floured surface into a 14" round. Transfer to a 9" pie dish. Lift up the edge and allow the dough to slump down into the dish. Trim. Leaving about 1" overhang. Fold overhang under and crimp edge. Chill in freezer 15 minutes.

5. When ready to cook, set the smoker to 350°F and preheat, lid closed for 15 minutes.

6. Line pie with parchment paper or heavy-duty foil, leaving a 1-1/2" overhang. Fill with pie weights or dried beans. Bake until crust is dry around the edge, about 20 minutes.

7. Remove paper and weights and bake until surface of the crust looks dry, 5-10 minutes.

8. Brush bottom and sides of crust with 1 beaten egg. Return to grill and bake until dry and set, about 3 minutes longer.

9. For the Pumpkin Maple Filling: Whisk together pumpkin puree, sour cream, bourbon, cinnamon, salt, ginger, nutmeg, allspice, mace (optional) and remaining 3 eggs in a large bowl; set aside.

10. Pour maple syrup and 2 tbsp sugar in a small saucepan. Scrape in the seeds from vanilla bean (reserve pod for another use) or add vanilla extract and bring syrup to a boil. Reduce heat to medium-high and simmer, stirring occasionally, until mixture is thickened and small puffs of steam start to release about 3 minutes.

11. Remove from heat and add cream in 3 additions, stirring with a wooden spoon after each addition until smooth. Gradually whisk hot maple cream into pumpkin mixture.

12. Place pie dish on a rimmed baking sheet and pour in pumpkin filling. Bake pie, rotating halfway through, until set around edge but center barely jiggles 50-60 minutes.

13. Transfer pie dish to a wire rack and let the pie cool. Slice and serve. Enjoy!

Strawberry Basil Daiquiri

Servings: 2
Cooking Time: 20 Minutes

Ingredients:
- 4 strawberries, stemmed
- 6 Tablespoon granulated sugar, divided
- 6 basil leaves
- 3 Ounce white rum
- 2 Ounce lime juice
- 1 Ounce Smoked Simple Syrup
- 2 fresh basil leaves, for garnish
- 2 lime slice, for garnish

Directions:
1. Supply your smoker with wood pellets and follow the start-up procedure. Preheat the grill, with the lid closed, to 375° F.

2. Cut strawberries in half and coat in 2 tablespoons granulated sugar. Place directly on grill grate and cook for 15 to 20 minutes. Remove from heat and cool. Grill: 375 °F

3. Add 1 tablespoon granulated sugar and basil leaves to shaking tin and lightly muddle. Add strawberries and muddle again.

4. Pour in white rum, lime juice and Smoked Simple Syrup. Shake with ice.

5. Strain contents into a chilled glass and garnish with large fresh basil leaf and sliced lime. Enjoy!

Lemon Strawberry Rhubarb Pie

Servings: 8
Cooking Time: 30 Minutes

Ingredients:

- 1/3 Cup Flour
- 1 Tbsp Lemon, Zest
- 1 Prepard Pie Shell, Deep
- 3 Stalks Rhubarb
- 2 1/2 Cups Strawberry
- 1 Cup Sugar

Directions:

1. Summer baking never has to stop when you can use your Wood Pellet Grill to bake anything from cookies to pie! In this recipe, we will show you how to bake a delicious barbecued strawberry rhubarb pie without turning your kitchen into an oven.
2. Supply your smoker with wood pellets and follow the start-up procedure. Preheat the grill, with the lid closed, to 400° F.
3. Slice rhubarb and strawberries into bite sized pieces. Combine sugar, flour and lemon zest with rhubarb and strawberries. Pour into prepared pie crust. Cover with top crust.
4. Bake in Grill for 1 hour or until crust is crispy.
5. Serve hot.

Focaccia

Servings: 6
Cooking Time: 40 Minutes

Ingredients:

- 1 Cup warm water (110°F to 115°F)
- 1/2 Ounce Yeast, active
- 1 Teaspoon sugar
- 2 1/2 Cup flour
- 1 Teaspoon salt
- 1/4 Cup extra-virgin olive oil
- 1 1/2 Teaspoon Italian herbs, dried
- 1/8 Teaspoon red pepper flakes
- As Needed coarse sea salt

Directions:

1. Measure the water in a glass-measuring cup. Stir in the yeast and sugar. Let rest for in a warm place. After 5 to 10 minutes, the mixture should be foamy, indicating the yeast is "alive." If it does not foam, discard it and start again.
2. Pour the water/yeast mixture in the bowl of a food processor. Add 1 cup of the flour as well as the salt and 1/4 cup of olive oil. Pulse several times to blend. Add the remaining flour, Italian herbs, and hot pepper flakes.
3. Process the dough until it's smooth and elastic and pulls away from the sides of the bowl, adding small amounts of flour or water through the feed tube if the dough is respectively too wet or too dry.
4. Let the dough rise in the covered food processor bowl in a warm place until doubled in bulk, about 1 hour5. Remove the dough from the food processor (it will deflate) and turn onto a lightly floured surface.
5. Oil two 8- to 9-inch round cake pans generously with olive oil. (Just pour a couple of glugs in and tilt the pan to spread the oil.) Divide the dough into two equal pieces, shape into disks, and put one in each prepared cake pan.
6. Oil the top of each disk with olive oil and dimple the dough with your fingertips. Sprinkle lightly with coarse salt, and if desired, additional dried Italian herbs.
7. Cover the focaccia dough with plastic wrap and let the dough rise in a warm place, about 45 minutes to an hour.

8. When ready to cook, start the smoker grill and set the temperature to 400F and preheat, lid closed, for 10 to 15 minutes.

9. Put the pans with the focaccia dough directly on the grill grate. Bake until the focaccia breads are light golden in color and baked through, 35 to 40 minutes, rotating the pans halfway through the baking time.

10. Let cool slightly before removing from the pans. Cut into wedges for serving.

Traeger Baked Focaccia

Servings: 4
Cooking Time: 40 Minutes

Ingredients:

- 2 1/2 Cup all-purpose flour
- 1 Cup warm water (110°F to 115°F)
- 1 Tablespoon instant yeast
- 1 Teaspoon sugar
- 1 Teaspoon salt
- 3 Tablespoon olive oil, plus more as needed
- 1 Tablespoon fresh herbs such as thyme, rosemary and sage
- 2 Tablespoon freshly grated Parmesan, optional
- flaky sea salt

Directions:

1. Place the flour, water, yeast, sugar, salt and oil in the bowl of a stand mixer and mix for 60 seconds. You may also use a food processor by adding the flour, sugar, salt and yeast to the bowl and process while streaming in the warm water followed by the olive oil. Process until combined and a ball forms.

2. Gently form the sticky dough into a ball, if needed, and place in a well-oiled 12 inch cast iron skillet. Drizzle the top of the dough with more olive oil. Cover with plastic wrap and a kitchen towel and let rise in a warm spot for 45 to 60 minutes.

3. After the dough has risen, press the dough to the edges of the pan and cover it again. Let rise for 15 minutes.

4. Supply your smoker with wood pellets and follow the start-up procedure. Preheat the grill, with the lid closed, to 375° F.

5. Uncover the dough and press it again to the edges of the pan using your fingertips to create divots.

6. Drizzle with olive oil, then sprinkle with herbs, Parmesan and flaky salt.

7. Bake it on the Traeger for 30 to 40 minutes, or until golden brown and cooked through. Allow it to cool slightly before removing from cast iron and slicing. Enjoy! Grill: 375 °F

Spiced Lemon Cherry Pie

Servings: 6-8
Cooking Time: 60 Minutes

Ingredients:

- 1/2 Teaspoon Cinnamon, Ground
- 1/2 Teaspoon Cloves, Ground
- 1/2 Cup Cornstarch
- 1 Pound Frozen Sweet Dark Cherries, Thawed
- 1 Teaspoon Water (Beaten With Egg) 1 Egg
- 1 Lemon, Juice
- 1 Lemon, Zest
- 2 Prepared Store Bought Or Homemade Pie Crust
- 1 Teaspoon Hickory Honey Sea Salt Seasoning
- 1 Cup Sugar, Granulated
- 1 Teaspoon Vanilla Extract

Directions:

1. In a large bowl, mix together the thawed cherries and their juices, sugar, cornstarch, lemon zest, lemon juice, cinnamon, clove, vanilla extract and Hickory Honey Sea Salt. Allow to sit for 30 minutes.

2. Flour a work surface and roll out one of the prepared pie crusts so that it fits a 9 inch pie tin. Fill with the cherry pie filling and refrigerate. When the pie is chilled, roll out the second pie crust, brush the edge of the first pie crust with the egg mixture, top with the second pie crust, crimp the edge with a fork, and chill. Alternatively, cut the second pie crust into strips and form a lattice pattern, attaching the strips with the egg mixture. Chill the pie for 15-30 minutes, or until the dough is very cold and firm. Brush the top of the pie with the remaining egg mixture.

3. Supply your smoker with wood pellets and follow the start-up procedure. Preheat the grill, with the lid closed, to 350° F and grill for 45 minutes to 1 hour, or until the pie crust is golden and firm and the filling is bubbly. Remove from the grill and allow to cool at room temperature for at least 4 hours to set the filling, then serve and enjoy!

Baked Wood-fired Pizza

Servings: 6
Cooking Time: 12 Minutes

Ingredients:
- 2/3 Cup warm water (110°F to 115°F)
- 2 1/2 Teaspoon active dry yeast
- 1/2 Teaspoon granulated sugar
- 1 Teaspoon kosher salt
- 1 Tablespoon oil
- 2 Cup all-purpose flour
- 1/4 Cup fine cornmeal
- 1 Large grilled portobello mushroom, sliced
- 1 Jar pickled artichoke hearts, drained and chopped
- 1 Cup shredded fontina cheese
- 1/2 Cup shaved Parmigiano-Reggiano cheese, divided
- To Taste Roasted Garlic, minced
- 1/4 Cup extra-virgin olive oil
- To Taste banana peppers

Directions:

1. In a glass bowl, stir together the warm water, yeast and sugar. Let stand until the mixture starts to foam, about 10 minutes. In a mixer, combine 1-3/4 cup flour, sugar and salt. Stir oil into the yeast mixture. Slowly add the liquid to the dry ingredients while slowly increasing the mixers speed until fully combined. The dough should be smooth and not sticky.

2. Knead the dough on a floured surface, gradually adding the remaining flour as needed to prevent the dough from sticking, until smooth, about 5 to 10 minutes.

3. Form the dough into a ball. Apply a thin layer of olive oil to a large bowl. Place the dough into the bowl and coat the dough ball with a small amount of olive oil. Cover and let rise in a warm place for about 1 hour or until doubled in size.

4. When ready to cook, set smoker temperature to 450°F and preheat, lid closed for 15 minutes.

5. Place a pizza stone in the grill while it preheats.

6. Punch the dough down and roll it out into a 12-inch circle on a floured surface.

7. Spread the cornmeal evenly on the pizza peel. Place the dough on the pizza peel and assemble the toppings evenly in the following order: olive

oil, roasted garlic, fontina, portobello, artichoke hearts, Parmigiano-Reggiano and banana peppers. 8. Carefully slide the assembled pizza from the pizza peel to the preheated pizza stone and bake until the crust is golden brown, about 10 to 12 minutes. Enjoy!

Vanilla Cheesecake Skillet Brownie

Servings: 2
Cooking Time: 30 Minutes

Ingredients:
- 1 Box Brownie Mix
- 1 Package Cream Cheese
- 2 Egg
- 1/2 Cup Oil
- 1 Can Pie Filling, Blueberry
- 1/2 Cup Sugar
- 1 Tsp Vanilla
- 1/4 Cup Water, Warm

Directions:

1. Combine all brownie ingredients and mix. In a separate bowl, combine cream cheese, sugar, egg and vanilla and mix until smooth. Grease skillets and pour in brownie batter. Top with cheesecake and cherry pie filling, using a knife to blend to give it that marbled look.

2. Supply your smoker with wood pellets and follow the start-up procedure. Preheat the grill, with the lid closed, to 350°F and bake for about 30 minutes.

3. Let cool for about 10 minutes and enjoy!

Savory Cheesecake With Bourbon Pecan Topping

Servings: 6

Cooking Time: 75 Minutes

Ingredients:
- Crust
- 12 ounce Oreos
- 6 ounce melted butter
- Filling
- 24 ounces cream cheese - room temperature
- 1 cup granulated sugar
- 3 tbs cornstarch
- 2 large eggs
- 2/3 cup heavy cream
- 1 tbs vanilla
- 1 1/2 tbs bourbon
- Topping
- 3 large eggs beaten
- 1/3 cup granulated sugar
- 1/3 cup brown sugar
- 8 tbsp corn syrup dark corn syrup recommended
- 2 tbsp bourbon
- 1/2 tbsp vanilla
- 1/8 tbsp salt
- 3/4 cup rough chopped pecans (smoked pecans recommended)

Directions:

1. Supply your smoker with wood pellets and follow the start-up procedure. Preheat the grill, with the lid closed, to 350 °F.

2. Wrap foil on the bottom and up the sides of a 9" spring-form pan (outside of pan).

3. Butter the bottom & insides of the pan.

4. Crust

5. Throw ingredients in a food processor until they are finely ground.

6. Spread in 9" cheesecake pan on bottom & about ½ way upsides.

7. Filling

8. Place 8 oz of cream cheese in mixer bowl with 1/3 of sugar & cornstarch.Mix until smooth andcreamy.

9. Add another 8 oz cream cheese andbeat until smooth, then add remaining cream cheese,beating until smooth.

10. Then mix in the rest of the sugar, bourbon & vanilla.

11. Add eggs one at a time beating well after each one.

12. Add the heavy cream and mix just until smooth. Reminder: Do not over mix.

13. Pour batter into the prepared crust.

14. Topping

15. Mix all together except pecans.

16. Sprinkle pecans on top of cheesecake batter.

17. Pour topping over cheesecake batter.

18. Place in a pan big enough to hold a spring-form pan. Pour boiling water in the roasting pan to come up about ½ way up the spring-form pan.

19. Bake at 350 °F for 75 minutes until the top just barely jiggles. Carefully take the pan out of water-bath and put on cooling rack.

20. Let cool for 2 hours in pan. After 2 hours put in fridge until totally chilled then serve.

Pizza Bites

Servings: 6
Cooking Time: 20 Minutes

Ingredients:
- 4 1/2 Cup Bread Flour
- 1 1/2 Tablespoon sugar
- 2 Teaspoon Instant Yeast
- 2 Teaspoon kosher salt
- 3 Tablespoon extra-virgin olive oil
- 15 Fluid Ounce Water, Lukewarm
- 8 Ounce Pepperoni, sliced
- 1 Cup pizza sauce
- 1 Cup mozzarella cheese
- 1 Whole egg, for egg wash
- 1 As Needed salt

Directions:
1. For the Pizza Dough: Combine flour, sugar, salt, and yeast in food processor. Pulse 3 to 4 times until incorporated evenly. Add olive oil and water. Run food processor until mixture forms ball that rides around the bowl above the blade, about 15 seconds. Continue processing 15 seconds longer.

2. Transfer dough ball to lightly floured surface and knead once or twice by hand until smooth ball is formed. Divide dough into three even parts and place each into a 1 gallon zip top bag. Place in refrigerator and allow to rise at least one day.

3. At least two hours before baking, remove dough from refrigerator and shape into balls by gathering dough towards bottom and pinching shut. Flour well and place each one in a separate medium mixing bowl. Cover tightly with plastic wrap and allow to rise at warm room temperature until roughly doubled in volume.

4. When ready to cook, set the grill temperature to 350°F and preheat, lid closed for 15 minutes.

5. After the first rise remove the dough from the fridge and let come to room temperature. Roll dough on a flat surface. Cut dough into long strips 3" wide by 18" long.

6. Slice pepperoni into strips.

7. In a medium bowl combine the pizza sauce, mozzarella and pepperoni.

8. Spoon 1 TBSP of the pizza filling onto the pizza dough every two inches, about halfway down the length of the dough. Dip a pastry brush into the egg wash and brush around pizza filling.

Fold the half side of the dough (without the pizza filling) over the other the half that contains the pizza filling.

9. Press down between each pizza bite slightly with your fingers. With a ravioli or pizza cutter, cut around each filling- creating a rectangle shape and sealing the crust in.

10. Transfer each pizza bite onto a parchment lined cookie sheet. Cover with a kitchen towel and let them rise for 30 minutes.

11. When ready to cook, preheat the grill to 350 ⊠ °F with the lid closed for 10-15 minutes.

12. Brush the bites with remaining egg wash, sprinkle with salt and place directly on the sheet tray. Bake 10-15 minutes until the exterior is golden brown.

13. Remove from grill and transfer to a serving dish. Serve with extra pizza sauce for dipping and enjoy!

Spiced Carrot Cake

Servings: 10
Cooking Time: 35 Minutes

Ingredients:
- 1/2 Cup Apple Sauce, Unsweetened
- 2 Tsp Baking Powder
- 1 Tsp Baking Soda
- 1 1/2 Cups Brown Sugar
- 1/2 Cup Butter, Room Temp
- 3/4 Cup Canola Oil
- 3 Cups Carrot, Grated
- 1 1/2 Tsp Cinnamon, Ground
- 2 (8-Ounce) Packages Cream Cheese, Room Temperature
- 4 Egg
- 2 Cups Flour, All-Purpose
- 1/2 Tsp Ginger, Ground
- 1/4 Tsp Nutmeg, Ground
- 1/2 Tsp Salt
- 1/2 Cup Sugar
- 3 Cups Sugar, Icing

Directions:
1. Supply your smoker with wood pellets and follow the start-up procedure. Preheat the grill, with the lid closed, to 350° F.

2. Line the bottom of 2 9-inch cake pans with parchment paper and spray the sides with cooking spray. Set aside.

3. In a large bowl, combine flour, baking powder and soda, spices and salt.

4. In a smaller bowl, combine oil, eggs, sugars, and applesauce and whisk together. Add carrots and stir until well combined.

5. Pour the wet ingredients into the dry. Stir until combined but take care not to over mix. Pour the batter evenly between the two cake pans. Bake for about 35 minutes in your Grill, rotating the cake pans halfway between the cook. Remove once a toothpick is inserted in the middle of the cake and comes out clean.

6. While the cake is cooling, prepare the frosting. Beat the cream cheese until smooth with a hand mixer. Add the butter and icing sugar and mix until fully combined.

7. On a clean plate or cake stand, place one half of the cake and top with a good layer of cream cheese frosting. Place the second half on top and cover with the remaining frosting. Icing tip: try not to lift your knife while icing. Instead make long, smooth strokes. Lifting the knife often make cause crumbs to get into your icing. Top with pecans if desired.

BEEF LAMB AND GAME RECIPES

Garlic Cheese Bacon Burger

Servings: 7
Cooking Time: 16 Minutes

Ingredients:
- 14 Bacon, Strip
- 3 Lbs Chuck Beef, Ground
- 7 Burger Buns
- 4 Cloves Garlic, Minced
- 1 Onion, Chopped
- 1 Tsp Pepper
- 8 Oz Pepper Jack Cheese, Sliced
- 2 Tomato, Sliced

Directions:
1. Supply your smoker with wood pellets and follow the start-up procedure. Preheat the grill, with the lid closed, to 400° F.
2. In a bowl, mix together the ground chuck, garlic, onion, and pepper. Separate the beef mixtures into about 7 equal bundles and form hamburger patties.
3. Brush the grate with oil, then add the patties and grill them on about 5-8 minutes on each side, or until desired doneness.
4. Remove the burgers from the grill. On the bottom half of the burger bun, add two tomato slices, top with a slice of pepper jack cheese, add the patty,
5. Place another slice of cheese on top, add two slices of bacon and top it off with the other half of the burger bun and serve.

Reverse-seared Steaks

Servings: 4
Cooking Time: 120 Minutes

Ingredients:
- 4 (4-ounce) sirloin steaks
- 2 tablespoons olive oil
- Salt
- Freshly ground black pepper
- 4 tablespoons butter

Directions:
1. Supply your smoker with wood pellets and follow the start-up procedure. Preheat the grill, with the lid closed, to 180°F.
2. Rub the steaks all over with olive oil and season both sides with salt and pepper.
3. Place the steaks directly on the grill grate and smoke until their internal temperature reaches 135°F. Remove the steaks from the grill.
4. Place a cast-iron skillet on the grill grate and increase the grill's temperature to 450°F.
5. Place the steaks in the skillet and top each with 1 tablespoon of butter. Cook the steaks until their internal temperature reaches 145°F, flipping once after 2 or 3 minutes. (I recommend reverse-searing over an open flame rather than in the cast-iron skillet, if your grill has that option.) Remove the steaks and serve immediately.

Georgia Smoked Onion Brisket Sandwich

Servings: 4
Cooking Time: 450 Minutes

Ingredients:
- ½ Cup Barbecue Sauce
- ¼ Cup Beef Broth
- 2 Tablespoons Bourbon
- 1, 3 Pound Brisket Flat, Trimmed

- 4 Kaiser Rolls
- ½ Cup Peach Preserves
- Sliced Pickles
- 4 Tablespoons Pulled Pork Rub
- Sliced White Onions

Directions:

1. Supply your smoker with wood pellets and follow the start-up procedure. Preheat the grill, with the lid closed, to 225° F.

2. Generously rub the brisket with the Pulled Pork Rub. Set aside.

3. In a bowl, mix together the barbecue sauce, peach preserves and bourbon. Set aside.

4. Place the brisket in the smoker and smoke for 5 hours, or until the internal temperature reaches 170°F. Once the brisket reaches temperature, remove from the smoker, place the brisket in foil and pour the beef broth over the top. Wrap the brisket tightly in aluminum foil and return to the smoker for another 2 hours, or until the internal temperature reaches 190°F.

5. Remove the brisket from the grill, unwrap the brisket, discard the foil, and brush the brisket generously with the peach glaze mixture. Place the brisket back on the smoker and smoke for 30 minutes, or until the brisket is shiny and glazed. Remove the brisket from the grill and rest for 10 minutes, covered in foil.

6. Once the brisket has rested, slice thickly against the grain and top the Kaiser rolls with the brisket slices, onion slices and pickle slices. Serve immediately.

The Boss Beef Burger

Servings: 10
Cooking Time: 85 Minutes

Ingredients:

- 4 Lbs Beef, Ground
- 1 Loaf Bread, Sourdough Round
- 1/2 Cup Butter
- Condiments (Ketchup, Mustard, Relish, Etc.)
- Lettuce
- 3 Cups Mushroom
- 3 Onion, Chopped
- Kansas City BBQ Sauce
- Mandarin Habanero Spice
- 1 Lbs Pork, Ground
- Red Onion, Chopped
- 1 Bag Shredded Cheddar Cheese
- Tomato, Sliced

Directions:

1. Supply your smoker with wood pellets and follow the start-up procedure. Preheat the grill, with the lid closed, to 300° F.

2. In a large bowl, mix together the ground beef, ground pork, eggs, barbecue sauce, and seasoning until combined. Do not over mix as this will cause the meat to be tough after cooking. Split the mixture into two equal parts.

3. Melt the butter in a pan over medium heat and sauté the onion mushrooms until golden.

4. In a cast iron pan, flatten one half of the meat mixture into the bottom, taking care to work meat slightly up the sides of the pan. Sprinkle in half of the bag of cheese. Pour in onion mixture and top with the rest of the cheese.

5. On a clean work surface, mold the second half of the meat mixture into a circle and cover the filling to complete the burger. Make sure that the top and bottom meat patties are secured together so that the filling cannot be seen.

6. Place the cast iron pan in the Grill for 1 hour - 1 hour 15 minutes, or until the internal temperature reaches 160°F. Crank up the to

"HIGH" and open the flame broiler. Flip the burger out of the cast iron pan onto the grates and sear each side for 5 minutes, to get those beautiful grill marks.

7. To serve: You can make an enormous burger like we did, or you can cut it like a pie into slices to be served on regular hamburger buns with your desired condiments.

Beer Braised Beef Sandwiches

Servings: 4
Cooking Time: 180 Minutes

Ingredients:

- 12 oz beer, porter or stout
- 1/2 black pepper
- 2 1/2 lbs chuck roast
- 4 hoagie rolls, sliced lengthwise
- 1/4 cup horseradish sauce
- 1 tbsp kosher salt
- 1 tbsp parsley, chopped
- 1 red onion, cut into thick rings
- 1/2 tbsp worcestershire sauce
- 1 yellow onion, cut into thick rings

Directions:

1. Supply your smoker with wood pellets and follow the start-up procedure. Preheat the grill, with the lid open, to 450° F. If using a gas or charcoal grill, set it up for high heat.
2. Set the chuck roast on a sheet tray, then season with salt and pepper. Place onions in a cast iron skillet or Dutch oven with a lid. Set aside.
3. Sear the chuck roast on the grill, 3 minutes per side, then transfer to the skillet set on top of the onions. Add the Worcestershire sauce and beer to the skillet, along the side of the roast. Cover and reduce the temperature to 325°F. Braise the roast for 2 ½ to 3 hours, until tender.

4. Remove the roast from the grill, add parsley, then pull apart and toss in reduced pan jus and onions.
5. Serve warm on hoagie rolls with horseradish sauce.

Rosemary Prime Rib

Servings: 8
Cooking Time: 60 Minutes

Ingredients:

- 1 (8 Lb) Prime Rib Roast
- 4 Tablespoon olive oil
- 4 Tablespoon tri-color peppercorns
- 3 Whole rosemary sprigs
- 3 Whole thyme sprigs
- 1/2 Cup garlic, minced
- 1/2 Cup Jacobsen Salt Co. Cherrywood Smoked Salt
- 4 Tablespoon Olive Oil

Directions:

1. Supply your smoker with wood pellets and follow the start-up procedure. Preheat the grill, with the lid closed, to 450° F.
2. Cut rib loin in half (roast halves separately for more controlled/even cooking.) Sear both halves in olive oil over very high heat until nice dark golden color.
3. Place tricolor peppercorns into a bag, crush pepper corns with a rolling pin.
4. Strip the leaves from the rosemary and thyme springs. Mix salt, crushed peppercorns, rosemary leaves, thyme leaves and garlic.
5. Pour olive oil over the rib loin and pour on the rub mix. Pat slightly to get it to stick to the meat.
6. Roast for 20-30 minutes on HIGH setting, then reduce heat to 300°F and roast for another

30 to 40 minutes or until a meat thermometer registers 125 degrees F for rare/medium rare (roast will continue to cook slightly after removing from the grill). Grill: 300 ˚F

7. Remove from the Traeger and let rest at least 20 minutes before slicing. Enjoy!

Garlic Pigs In A Blanket

Servings: 10
Cooking Time: 15 Minutes

Ingredients:
- 1 Crescent Dough, Can
- 1 Egg
- 1 Tsp Garlic, Minced
- 20 Hot Dog, Mini
- 1/4 Cup Mustard, Dijon
- 1 Tbsp Onion, Diced
- 2 Tbsp Poppy Seeds
- 1 Tsp Salt, Coarse

Directions:

1. Supply your smoker with wood pellets and follow the start-up procedure. Preheat the grill, with the lid closed, to 350˚ F. Combine the poppy seeds, dried minced onion, minced garlic, and salt in a bowl.

2. Unroll the crescent roll dough, pull apart the triangles and slice each segment into three little triangle pieces. Try to get 3 strips for each roll for the mini hot dogs.

3. After the strips are cut, spread some Dijon mustard on each piece of dough. Roll the dough around mini hot dogs. Lay the pigs in a blanket on a greased cookie sheet. Brush with egg wash and sprinkle with the prepared seasoning.

4. Bake for 15 minutes, serve hot and enjoy!

Smoked Spiced Rump Roast

Servings: 8
Cooking Time: 60 Minutes

Ingredients:
- 3 pounds rump roast (or bottom round roast)
- 1 ½ teaspoons coarse ground pepper
- 1 teaspoon kosher salt
- ¼ teaspoon garlic powder
- ¼ teaspoon onion powder

Directions:

1. Supply your smoker with wood pellets and follow the start-up procedure. Preheat the grill, with the lid closed, to 250 ˚F.

2. Combine the seasonings in a small bowl and coat the rump roast evenly with seasonings on all sides.

3. Place roast into the smoker.

4. Cook for 1 hour and 45 minutes, or until the internal temperature reaches 135 degrees (or your desired level of doneness; rare: 135 ˚F, medium rare: 145 ˚F, medium: 155 ˚F, well done: 170 ˚F)

5. Remove rump roast from the smoker and let it rest for 10 minutesbefore slicing.

6. Slice thinly and serve.

Smoked Black Pepper Beef Ribs

Servings: 4-6
Cooking Time: 330 Minutes

Ingredients:
- 1/4 Cup Hot Sauce
- Kosher Salt
- Coarse Black Pepper
- Your Favorite Beef Rib Rub Or Sweet Heat Rub
- 4 Pound Rib(S)

Directions:

1. Supply your smoker with wood pellets and follow the start-up procedure. Preheat the grill, with the lid closed, to 250° F.

2. Peel the membrane off the bone side and remove excess fat.

3. Rub the ribs down with hot sauce and season generously with Sweet Heat, salt, and pepper.

4. Place the ribs on the grill. Then, insert your meat probe before closing the lid to cook.

5. Check on your ribs after 3-4 hours. If one side is cooking faster than the other, rotate them.

6. Once the beef reaches 195°F, start probe testing the ribs for doneness. Because the finished temperature can vary, do a check with each time the temperature increases by 3°F.

7. To probe test: insert the meat probe vertically in between the bones to push through the second membrane on the bottom. The meat should have a consistent butter like tenderness throughout the rack with a final internal temp ranging from 200°F – 205°F.

8. Once the ribs finish cooking, remove from the grill to let them rest.

9. To let the ribs rest: wrap them tightly in foil. Then, wrap in a towel and place in a dry, empty cooler for 1 hour.

10. Slice between the bones to serve and enjoy!

Baked Ziti With Italian Sausage

Servings: 6
Cooking Time: 20 Minutes

Ingredients:

- 1 Pound Ziti, cooked 1 minute less than directions, and dried
- 1 Jar Spaghetti Sauce
- 1 Teaspoon garlic, minced
- 1 Pinch red pepper flakes
- 1 Pound Italian Sausage, cooked
- salt and pepper
- 2 Cup Mozzarella Cheese, Grated
- 1/4 Cup Parmesan cheese

Directions:

1. Supply your smoker with wood pellets and follow the start-up procedure. Preheat the grill, with the lid closed, to 450° F.

2. In a large bowl, pour your spaghetti sauce over the cooked pasta, add garlic, red pepper flakes, and salt and pepper to taste. Toss. Fold the sausage into the pasta mixture.

3. Coat a 9 x 13 x 2-inch baking dish with nonstick cooking spray.

4. Pour half of the pasta mixture into your prepared baking dish. Sprinkle with half of the mozzarella. Pour remaining pasta into the dish, smooth out the top and add the remaining mozzarella.

5. Bake in Traeger until cheese is golden brown and bubbly, about 20 minutes.

6. Remove and sprinkle with parmesan cheese. Enjoy!

Traeger Blt Burgers

Servings: 6
Cooking Time: 45 Minutes

Ingredients:

- 2 Pound ground chuck, 80% lean
- Beef Rub
- 1/2 Cup mayonnaise
- 1/3 Cup 'Que BBQ Sauce
- 1 pickle juice
- 1 Pound Pastrami, Sliced
- 8 Slices Cheese, sharp cheddar
- 8 hamburger buns

- Desired Toppings: Lettuce, Tomatoes, Red Onions, Etc.

Directions:

1. Supply your smoker with wood pellets and follow the start-up procedure. Preheat the grill, with the lid closed, to 180° F.

2. Divide ground beef into 8 equal sized patties; season with Traeger's Beef Rub. Place directly on the grill grate, close the lid, and smoke for 30 minutes. Grill: 180 °F

3. While the burgers smoke, make the fry sauce. In a small bowl, combine the mayo, BBQ sauce, and pickle juice. Stir to combine, cover, and keep in the refrigerator until ready to use.

4. Remove the burgers from the grill and increase the temperature to 450 degrees F. Allow the grill to preheat for 10-15 minutes before returning the burgers to the grill grate. Grill: 450 °F

5. Cook for 4-5 minutes on one side, then flip burgers. When you flip the burgers, add the pastrami to the grill in 8 individually portioned piles. Close the lid and cook for an additional 4-5 minutes. Grill: 450 °F

6. Carefully transfer the pastrami to the top of the burgers and place a slice of cheese on each. If desired, you can also add the buns to the grill so they can get toasted. Close the lid again and cook until the cheese is melted and the burgers reach a desired level of doneness. The recommended internal temperature for a well-done burger is 175 degrees F.

7. Transfer the pastrami topped burgers to the bottom bun. Slather the top bun with the fry sauce, adorn with the burger toppings of your choosing and serve. Enjoy!

London Broil

Servings: 4
Cooking Time: 16 Minutes

Ingredients:

- 1 (1½- to 2-pound) London broil or top round steak
- ¼ cup soy sauce
- 2 tablespoons white wine
- 2 tablespoons extra-virgin olive oil
- ¼ cup chopped scallions
- 2 tablespoons packed brown sugar
- 2 garlic cloves, minced
- 2 teaspoons red pepper flakes
- 1 teaspoon freshly ground black pepper

Directions:

1. Using a meat mallet, pound the steak lightly all over on both sides to break down its fibers and tenderize. You are not trying to pound down the thickness

2. In a medium bowl, make the marinade by combining the soy sauce, white wine, olive oil, scallions, brown sugar, garlic, red pepper flakes, and black pepper

3. Put the steak in a shallow plastic container with a lid and pour the marinade over the meat. Cover and refrigerate for at least 4 hours.

4. Remove the steak from the marinade, shaking off any excess, and discard the marinade

5. Supply your smoker with wood pellets and follow the start-up procedure. Preheat, with the lid closed, to 350°F6. Place the steak directly on the grill, close the lid, and smoke for 6 minutes. Flip, then smoke with the lid closed for 6 to 10 minutes more, or until a meat thermometer inserted in the meat reads 130°F for medium-rare

6. Let the steak rest for about 10 minutes before slicing and serving. The meat's temperature will rise by about 5 degrees while it rests

Garlic Parmesan Grilled Filet Mignon

Servings: 2
Cooking Time: 10 Minutes

Ingredients:

- 4 filet mignon steaks
- 1 Teaspoon salt
- 1 Teaspoon black pepper
- 1 Teaspoon garlic salt
- 1 Cup Parmesan cheese
- 4 garlic
- 1 Tablespoon Dijon mustard

Directions:

1. Supply your smoker with wood pellets and follow the start-up procedure. Preheat the grill, with the lid closed, to High heat.

2. While the grill is heating up, season the filets with salt, pepper, and garlic salt. Also mince your garlic and chop your Parmesan so it's fine, and combine.

3. When the grill reaches temperature, place filets on the grill and cook for 4 minutes on each side. After 8 minutes total, spread the filets with the Dijon mustard and dip in the minced garlic and Parmesan cheese mixture and place back on the grill for another 1-2 minutes or until the cheese is melted.

4. Let rest for 5 minutes and serve. Enjoy!

Bacon-wrapped Elk Steaks

Servings: 2
Cooking Time: 15 Minutes

Ingredients:

- 1/4 Cup red wine
- 2 Tablespoon soy sauce
- 2 Tablespoon honey
- 2 Clove garlic, minced
- 1/4 Teaspoon freshly cracked black pepper
- 2 Tablespoon rosemary, chopped
- 1/8 Teaspoon red pepper flakes
- 2 Pound Elk Steak
- 1/2 Pound thick-cut bacon

Directions:

1. Make the marinade by whisking together the wine, soy sauce, honey, minced garlic cloves, black pepper, chopped rosemary and red pepper flakes. Slowly drizzle in the olive oil while whisking

2. Add the elk steaks into the marinade and marinate overnight, up to a day or two.

3. Supply your smoker with wood pellets and follow the start-up procedure. Preheat the grill, with the lid closed, to 450° F.

4. Take the steaks out of the marinade; wrap each steak with several pieces of bacon and secure with toothpicks.

5. Place the bacon-wrapped elk steaks directly on the grill grate and cook for 10 to 15 minutes, or until it has reached an internal temperature of 135 degrees F. Rotate halfway through for a good caramelized exterior. Enjoy!

Smoked Spiced Pulled Beef Chuck Roast

Servings: 6-8
Cooking Time: 360 Minutes

Ingredients:

- 1 chuck roast (3-4 pounds)
- 1 yellow or white onion (sliced)
- 3 cups beef stock (divided use)
- SIMPLE BEEF RUB
- 2 Tablespoons kosher salt
- 2 Tablespoons coarse black pepper

- 2 Tablespoons garlic powder

Directions:

1. Supply your smoker with wood pellets and follow the start-up procedure. Preheat the grill, with the lid closed, to 225 °F.

2. Combine all of the ingredients for the rub in a small bowl and rub liberally onto your beef roast, using your hands to press the rub into every surface of the meat.

3. Put the roast directly on your grill grate, fat-side up, and cook for 3 hours. Spray with 1 cup of the beef stock every hour (reserve the other 2 cups of stock).

4. Turn up the heat after 3 hours. Place the sliced onions in the bottom of a large disposable aluminum foil pan and pour the remaining 2 cups of stock in the bottom of the pan. Transfer the roast into the pan on top of the onions and place the pan into the grill.

5. Increase your grill temperature to 250 degrees F, and cook until the internal temperature reaches 165 degrees F (about 3 more hours).

6. Cover the pan tightly with aluminum foil once your roast hits 165 degrees F, and continue cooking until thermometer inserted in the thickest part of the meat reads 200 to 202 degrees F (this step can take another 3 hours). Every roast will be done at a slightly different temperature, so look for your probe to slide into the meat like it is sliding into softened butter.

7. Remove the pan from the smoker and let rest for a few minutes. Separate the roast from the cooking liquid. Shred the roast and separate the fat from the cooking liquid. Moisten the roast with the remaining cooking liquid, or make it into jus for dipping, or turn it into gravy.

Wagyu Corned Beef Hash

Servings: 8

Cooking Time: 360 Minutes

Ingredients:

- 2 1/2 Pound Wagyu Corned Beef Roast
- 2 red bell pepper, diced
- 1 green bell pepper, diced
- 2 Pound Southern Hash Brown
- 3 Cup shredded cheddar cheese
- 2 Tablespoon kosher salt
- 2 Tablespoon black pepper
- 7 eggs
- 1/2 Cup whole milk

Directions:

1. Corned Beef: Corned beef needs to be cooked at least one day prior to making the hash.

2. Supply your smoker with wood pellets and follow the start-up procedure. Preheat the grill, with the lid closed, to 275° F.

3. Rinse the corned beef and place on grill. Cook for 4 to 4.5 hours. Wrap in a double layer of heavy duty tin foil and put back on the grill. Grill: 275 °F

4. Cook meat until it reaches an internal temperature of 204 degrees F. This should take 2-3 more hours. Let vent for 2 hours and place in fridge. Refrigerate overnight. Grill: 275 °F Probe: 204 °F

5. Corned Beef Hash: Chop and cook the peppers in cast iron for 20 minutes.

6. When ready to cook, start the Traeger and set the temperature to 350 degrees F and preheat, lid closed, for 10 minutes. Grill: 350 °F

7. Cut the corned beef into bite-sized pieces. Combine the hash browns, corned beef, bell peppers, cheese, salt and pepper. Mix well and place in a 9x13 baking dish.

8. Mix eggs and milk in a separate bowl. Pour over the top of the hash brown mixture.

9. Cover with foil and set on the grill for a 1.5 hours. The internal temperature should reach 165 degrees F. Serve and enjoy! Grill: 350 ℉ Probe: 165 ℉

Naked Juicy Lucy Burgers With Special Sauce

Servings: 4
Cooking Time: 40 Minutes

Ingredients:
- 2lb (1kg) ground beef (80/20), preferably chuck, well chilled
- 1 tbsp Worcestershire sauce or liquid aminos
- 6oz (170g) grated Cheddar, pepper Jack, or another melting cheese
- coarse salt
- freshly ground black pepper
- for the sauce
- ¼ cup reduced-fat mayo
- ¼ cup yellow mustard
- ¼ cup ketchup
- ¼ cup Heinz 57 sauce
- 2 tbsp sweet pickle relish
- for serving
- sliced tomatoes
- sliced sweet onions
- lettuce leaves
- cooked bacon strips
- Pickles

Directions:
1. Supply your smoker with wood pellets and follow the start-up procedure. Preheat the grill, with the lid closed, to 225° F.

2. In a small bowl, make the sauce by combining the ingredients. Transfer the sauce to a serving bowl. Cover and refrigerate until ready to use. (Leftover sauce will keep for several weeks.)

3. Place the ground beef in a large bowl and add the Worcestershire sauce. Wet your hands with cold water and lightly mix. Divide the mixture into 8 equal-sized balls. Flatten each ball into a round patty.

4. Place 4 patties on a rimmed sheet pan. Mound an equal amount of cheese in the middle of each patty, leaving a meat border. Place a patty on top of each cheese mound. Rewet your hands with cold water and press and pinch the edges of patties together to form a tight seal. (You don't want the cheese to leak out.) Season on both sides with salt and pepper.

5. Place the patties on the grate and smoke for 30 minutes. Transfer the burgers to a clean plate.

6. Raise the temperature to 450°F (232°C). Return the burgers to the grate and sear them until the burgers reach an internal temperature of 160°F (71°C), about 3 to 4 minutes per side, turning once.

7. Transfer the burgers to a platter and let rest for 3 minutes. Serve with the special sauce and the suggested accompaniments.

Greek Leg Of Lamb

Servings: 12-16
Cooking Time: 25 Minutes

Ingredients:
- 2 tablespoons finely chopped fresh rosemary
- 1 tablespoon ground thyme
- 5 garlic cloves, minced
- 2 tablespoons sea salt
- 1 tablespoon freshly ground black pepper
- Butcher's string
- 1 whole boneless (6- to 8-pound) leg of lamb

- ¼ cup extra-virgin olive oil
- 1 cup red wine vinegar
- ½ cup canola oil

Directions:

1.   In a small bowl, combine the rosemary, thyme, garlic, salt, and pepper; set aside.

2.   Using butcher's string, tie the leg of lamb into the shape of a roast. Your butcher should also be happy to truss the leg for you.

3.   Rub the lamb generously with the olive oil and season with the spice mixture. Transfer to a plate, cover with plastic wrap, and refrigerate for 4 hours.

4.   Remove the lamb from the refrigerator but do not rinse.

5.   Supply your smoker with wood pellets and follow the start-up procedure. Preheat, with the lid closed, to 325°F.

6.   In a small bowl, combine the red wine vinegar and canola oil for basting.

7.   Place the lamb directly on the grill, close the lid, and smoke for 20 to 25 minutes per pound (depending on desired doneness), basting with the oil and vinegar mixture every 30 minutes. Lamb is generally served medium-rare to medium, so it will be done when a meat thermometer inserted in the thickest part reads 140°F to 145°F.

8.   Let the lamb rest for about 15 minutes before slicing to serve.

Steak Tips With Mashed Potatoes

Servings: 4-6
Cooking Time: 60 Minutes

Ingredients:

- 1 Cup Beef Broth
- 1 Stick (Room Temperature) Butter, Unsalted
- 2 Tablespoon Flour, All-Purpose
- 1 Tablespoon Java Chophouse Seasoning
- 4 Tablespoon Java Chophouse Seasoning, Divided
- 2 Pounds Medium Russet Potatoes, Peeled And Cut (Large Chunks)
- 2 Pounds Strip Sirloin
- 1/2 To 1 Cup Whole Milk, Warm

Directions:

1.   For the mashed potatoes: add the potatoes to a large pot and add enough cold water to cover the potatoes. Bring to a simmer over medium heat until the potatoes are tender enough to be pierced with a fork, about 40 minutes. Drain the potatoes.

2.   Add the potatoes to a large mixing bowl. Add the butter, 1 tablespoon of Java Chop House and ½ cup of warm milk. Mash until smooth and lump free. If potatoes are too thick, add more milk, a tablespoon at a time, until you reach your desired consistency.

3.   For the steak tips: Supply your smoker with wood pellets and follow the start-up procedure. Preheat the grill, with the lid closed, to 350° F. Season the steaks generously on both sides with 2 tablespoons of Java Chop House seasoning and grill for 8-10 minutes per side. When steaks are done, remove from grill, allow to rest for 15 minutes, then cut into chunks.

4.   While the steak is resting, add the butter to a small saucepan over low heat. Once the butter is melted, whisk in the flour and cook for 2 minutes until the flour smells toasted. Slowly whisk in the beef broth and remaining 2 tablespoons of Java Chop House seasoning and cook the gravy over low heat until thickened. Remove from heat and toss the steak tips in the gravy.

5.   Serve steak tips over mashed potatoes. Enjoy!

Lemon Tomahawk Steak

Servings: 2 – 4

Cooking Time: 215 Minutes

Ingredients:

- Apple Corer Or Metal Spoon
- 3 Lbs Gala Apples
- 1 Lemon
- Chop House Steak Rub
- 1 Tbsp   Tennessee Apple Butter Rub
- Sugar
- 4 Cups Water

Directions:

1. Supply your smoker with wood pellets and follow the start-up procedure. Preheat the grill, with the lid closed, to 400° F. If using a gas or charcoal grill, set heat to medium-high heat.

2. Core and halve the apples. Place apples skin-side down on a sheet tray and season with Tennessee Apple Butter and set aside.

3. In a cast iron pot, combine the apple cores with the juice and zest from one lemon. Cover the mixture with water, transfer to the grill and bring to a boil. Reduce heat to 225° F. Place the apples directly on the grill grate (skin-side down) and cook for 1 hour.

4. After 1 hour, remove cast iron pot from the grill. Strain liquid, discard cores, return liquid to pot, and whisk in sugar. Cover with lid and return to grill. Allow to simmer for another hour.

5. Add smoked apples to the pot and continue to simmer for 20 minutes. Remove pot from grill and purée apple mixture in a blender. Pour apple purée back into pot and return to grill. Increase heat to 375° F and simmer for 20 minutes. Remove from grill and allow to cool slightly.

6. Reduce heat on grill to 225° F. Season the tomahawk steak with   Chop House Steak Rub on both sides. Place the steak on the grill grates, insert a temperature probe, and grill, undisturbed, for 45 minutes, or until the steak reaches an internal temperature of 120°F

7. Remove steak from grill and set aside. Open the Sear Slide on your   and increase temperature to 400°F. Return tomahawk to grill and sear over open flames, about 2-3 minutes per side.

8. Pull the steak off the grill and allow it to rest for 10 minutes. Ladle reserved apple butter over steak and serve.

Vietnamese Beef Jerky

Servings: 6

Cooking Time: 240 Minutes

Ingredients:

- 2 Pound lean bottom round, rump roast or sirloin
- 2 Large garlic, roughly chopped
- 1 Stalk fresh lemongrass, trimmed and white parts thinly sliced
- 1 1/2 inch fresh ginger, peeled and roughly chopped
- 1/2 Cup soy sauce or Bragg Liquid Aminos
- 3 Tablespoon water
- 3 Tablespoon sugar
- 2 Tablespoon fish sauce
- 2 Teaspoon red chile flakes, or more to taste
- 1/2 Teaspoon pink curing salt (optional)

Directions:

1. Remove any visible fat from the meat and slice it into thin strips against the grain with a sharp chef's knife. (This is easier if the meat is partially frozen.) Transfer to a large, sturdy resealable bag.

2. Make the Marinade: In a blender jar or food processor bowl, combine the garlic, lemongrass,

ginger, soy sauce, water, sugar, fish sauce, chile flakes and pink curing salt, if using. Pulse until relatively smooth.

3. Pour over the meat and massage the bag so the meat strips are evenly coated with the marinade. Refrigerate for at least 8 hours, or overnight. Turn the bag once or twice to redistribute the juices.

4. Supply your smoker with wood pellets and follow the start-up procedure. Preheat the grill, with the lid closed, to 165° F.

5. Drain the meat (discard the marinade) and pat dry with paper towels. Arrange the meat strips directly on the grill grate, perpendicular to the bars in a single layer. If you like your jerky spicy, feel free to lightly sprinkle additional red chile flakes on the meat.

6. Smoke the jerky, turning once, until the jerky is dry, but still pliant, about 4 to 6 hours. Grill: 165 °F

7. Let cool completely, then transfer to a clean resealable bag. Store in the refrigerator for the longest shelf life. The jerky can also be frozen. Enjoy!

Braised Mediterranean Beef Brisket

Servings: 8
Cooking Time: 720 Minutes

Ingredients:
- 3 Tablespoon dried rosemary
- 2 Tablespoon ground cumin seeds
- 2 Tablespoon Coriander, Dried
- 1 Tablespoon dried oregano
- 2 Teaspoon ground cinnamon
- 1/2 Teaspoon salt
- 8 Pound beef brisket

- 1 Cup beef stock

Directions:

1. For a 6 to 8 lb brisket, plan for 8 to 12 hours of cook time, roughly 90 minutes per pound. A remote probe thermometer is critical to use for brisket.

2. Mix all seasoning together and coat brisket liberally. Wrap in plastic wrap. Let the wrapped brisket sit 12 to 24 hours in the refrigerator. Allow plenty of time for cooking.

3. Supply your smoker with wood pellets and follow the start-up procedure. Preheat the grill, with the lid closed, to 180° F.

4. Place brisket fat side down on the grill grate, insert thermometer probe and smoke for 4 hours.

5. After 4 hours, turn grill up to 250°F and preheat. Grill: 250 °F Probe: 250 °F

6. When internal meat temperature reaches 160°F, remove brisket from the grill and wrap in foil along with beef stock - DO NOT remove thermometer probe.

7. Place foiled brisket back on grill and cook until internal temperature reaches 204°F. Grill: 250 °F Probe: 204 °F

8. Remove brisket and allow it to rest in the foil for at least 30 minutes before slicing. Enjoy!

Smoked Bourbon Jerky

Servings: 6
Cooking Time: 360 Minutes

Ingredients:
- 3 Pound flank steak
- 1 Cup bourbon
- 1/2 Cup brown sugar
- 1/4 Cup Jerky Rub
- 1 Can chipotle peppers in adobo sauce
- 3 Tablespoon Worcestershire sauce

- 1/2 Cup apple cider vinegar

Directions:

1. Roll flank steak up parallel to the grain. Slice, with the grain, into 1/4 inch thick slices.

2. Combine all ingredients for marinade in a medium bowl and mix well. Place sliced flank steak in a large zip top bag and pour marinade over steak.

3. Place in refrigerator and marinate overnight.

4. Supply your smoker with wood pellets and follow the start-up procedure. Preheat the grill, with the lid closed, to 180° F.

5. Remove flank from the marinade, discard marinade and lay slices on a jerky rack or directly on the grill grate. Grill: 180 °F

6. Smoke for about 6 hours or until jerky has dried out but is still pliable. Grill: 180 °F

7. Remove from grill and let cool at room temperature, lightly covered for 1 hour.

8. Store in an airtight container or zip top bag in the refrigerator. Enjoy!

Texas Smoked Beer Leftover Rib Meat

Servings: 4
Cooking Time: 30 Minutes

Ingredients:
- 1 Can Beer, Any Brand
- 1 Can Black Beans, Rinsed And Drained
- 1 Tablespoon Chili Powder
- 1 Can Corn Kernels, Drained
- 1/2 Teaspoon Cumin
- 1 Can Kidney Beans, Drained And Rinsed
- 2 Cups Pulled From The Bone Leftover Rib Meat
- 2 Tablespoons Louisiana Grills Pulled Pork Rub

- 1 Tablespoon Olive Oil
- 1 Can Tomato Sauce
- 1/2 White Onion, Diced

Directions:

1. Supply your smoker with wood pellets and follow the start-up procedure. Preheat the grill, with the lid closed, to 250° F. In a pan sauté your diced onions in olive oil and 1 tablespoon of beer until they turn a mild yellow color.

2. In the disposable aluminum pan, combine the sautéed onions and the rest of the ingredients, including the leftover beef rib meat.

3. Mix the ingredients well and cover tightly with aluminum foil.

4. Place on the grill and close the lid. Let smoke for 2 - 3 hours or until the chili is bubbling and tender.

Pastrami

Servings: 6-8
Cooking Time: 960 Minutes

Ingredients:
- 1 (8-pound) corned beef brisket
- 2 tablespoons yellow mustard
- 1 batch Espresso Brisket Rub
- Worcestershire Mop and Spritz, for spritzing

Directions:

1. Supply your smoker with wood pellets and follow the start-up procedure. Preheat the grill, with the lid closed, to 225°F.

2. Coat the brisket all over with mustard and season it with the rub. Using your hands, work the rub into the meat. Pour the mop into a spray bottle.

3. Place the brisket directly on the grill grate and smoke until its internal temperature reaches 195°F, spritzing it every hour with the mop.

4. Pull the corned beef brisket from the grill and wrap it completely in aluminum foil or butcher paper. Place the wrapped brisket in a cooler, cover the cooler, and let it rest for 1 or 2 hours.

5. Remove the corned beef from the cooler and unwrap it. Slice the corned beef and serve.

Grilled Bell Pepper Flank Steak Fajitas

Servings: 1
Cooking Time: 30 Minutes

Ingredients:
- 1 Green Bell Pepper, Sliced
- 3 Tbsp Olive Oil
- 1 Onion, Diced
- Sweet Heat Rub
- 1 Red Bell Peppers, Sliced
- 1 -16Oz Steak, Flank
- 8 Tortilla, Corn
- 1 Yellow Bell Pepper, Sliced

Directions:
1. Rub flank steak with 1 tbsp olive oil and Sweet Heat Rub Grill seasoning. Cover and marinate in the refrigerator for 1 hour.

2. Lightly brush peppers and onion with olive oil.

3. Supply your smoker with wood pellets and follow the start-up procedure. Preheat the grill, with the lid closed, to 400° F. Place pepper and onion on grill and cook 5 minutes per side. Watch carefully to ensure the peppers and onion do not burn.

4. Remove peppers and onion from grill and toss lightly with remaining olive oil in a medium sized bowl. Transfer peppers and onions to a cutting board and slice into strips. Set aside.

5. Place flank steak directly on grill. Cook until medium rare (an internal temperature of 165°F).

6. Remove flank steak from the grill and transfer to cutting board. Let meat rest for 5 minutes, then slice against the grain into strips.

7. Place flank steak, peppers, and onions in a platter and serve immediately with warm tortillas, salsa, guacamole, sour cream, shredded cheese, thinly sliced iceberg lettuce, or your favorite fajita toppings.

Chicken Wings With Teriyaki Glaze

Servings: 4

Cooking Time: 50 Minutes

Ingredients:

- 16 large chicken wings, about 3lb (1.4kg) total
- 1 to 1½ tbsp toasted sesame oil
- for the glaze
- ½ cup light soy sauce or tamari
- ¼ cup sake or sugar-free dark-colored soda
- ¼ cup light brown sugar or low-carb substitute
- 2 tbsp mirin or 1 tbsp honey
- 1 garlic clove, peeled, minced or grated
- 2 tsp minced fresh ginger
- 1 tsp cornstarch mixed with 1 tbsp distilled water (optional)
- for serving
- 1 tbsp toasted sesame seeds
- 2 scallions, trimmed, white and green parts sliced sharply diagonally

Directions:

1. Supply your smoker with wood pellets and follow the start-up procedure. Preheat the grill, with the lid closed, to 350° F.

2. Place the chicken wings in a large bowl, add the sesame oil, and turn the wings to coat thoroughly.

3. Place the wings on the grate at an angle to the bars. Grill for 20 minutes and then turn. Continue to cook until the wings are nicely browned and the meat is no longer pink at the bone, about 20 minutes more.

4. To make the glaze, in a saucepan on the stovetop over medium-high heat, combine the ingredients and bring the mixture to a boil. Reduce the glaze by 1/3, about 6 to 8 minutes. If you prefer your glaze to be glossy and thick, add the cornstarch and water mixture to the glaze and cook until it coats the back of a spoon, about 1 to 2 minutes more.

5. Transfer the wings to an aluminum foil roasting pan. Pour the glaze over them, turning to coat thoroughly. Place the pan on the grate and cook the wings until the glaze sets, about 5 to 10 minutes.

6. Transfer the wings to a platter. Scatter the sesame seeds and scallions over the top. Serve with plenty of napkins.

Bacon-wrapped Jalapeño Poppers

Servings: 12

Cooking Time: 30 Minutes

Ingredients:

- 8 ounces cream cheese, softened
- ½ cup shredded Cheddar cheese
- ¼ cup chopped scallions
- 1 teaspoon chipotle chile powder or regular chili powder
- 1 teaspoon garlic powder
- 1 teaspoon salt
- 18 large jalapeño peppers, stemmed, seeded, and halved lengthwise
- 1 pound bacon (precooked works well)

Directions:

1. Supply your smoker with wood pellets and follow the start-up procedure. Preheat, with the

lid closed, to 350°F. Line a baking sheet with aluminum foil.

2. In a small bowl, combine the cream cheese, Cheddar cheese, scallions, chipotle powder, garlic powder, and salt.

3. Stuff the jalapeño halves with the cheese mixture.

4. Cut the bacon into pieces big enough to wrap around the stuffed pepper halves.

5. Wrap the bacon around the peppers and place on the prepared baking sheet.

6. Put the baking sheet on the grill grate, close the lid, and smoke the peppers for 30 minutes, or until the cheese is melted and the bacon is cooked through and crisp.

7. Let the jalapeño poppers cool for 3 to 5 minutes. Serve warm.

Bacon Pork Pinwheels (kansas Lollipops)

Servings: 4-6
Cooking Time: 20 Minutes

Ingredients:
- 1 Whole Pork Loin, boneless
- To Taste salt and pepper
- To Taste Greek Seasoning
- 4 Slices bacon
- To Taste The Ultimate BBQ Sauce

Directions:

1. When ready to cook, start the smoker and set temperature to 500F. Preheat, lid closed, for 10 to 15 minutes.

2. Trim pork loin of any unwanted silver skin or fat. Using a sharp knife, cut pork loin length wise, into 4 long strips.

3. Lay pork flat, then season with salt, pepper and Cavender's Greek Seasoning.

4. Flip the pork strips over and layer bacon on unseasoned side. Begin tightly rolling the pork strips, with bacon being rolled up on the inside.

5. Secure a skewer all the way through each pork roll to secure it in place. Set the pork rolls down on grill and cook for 15 minutes.

6. Brush BBQ Sauce over the pork. Turn each skewer over, then coat the other side. Let pork cook for another 5-10 minutes, depending on thickness of your pork. Enjoy!

Bayou Wings With Cajun Rémoulade

Servings: 8
Cooking Time: 40 Minutes

Ingredients:
- 16 large whole chicken wings or 32 drumettes and flats, about 3lb (1.4kg) total
- for the rub
- 1 tbsp kosher salt
- 1 tsp freshly ground black pepper
- 1 tsp paprika
- ½ tsp ground cayenne, plus more
- ½ tsp garlic powder
- ½ tsp celery salt
- ½ tsp dried thyme
- 2 tbsp vegetable oil
- for the rémoulade
- 1¼ cups reduced-fat mayo
- ¼ cup Creole-style or whole grain mustard
- 2 tbsp horseradish
- 2 tbsp pickle relish
- 1 tbsp freshly squeezed lemon juice
- 1 tsp paprika, plus more
- 1 tsp hot sauce, plus more
- 1 tsp Worcestershire sauce
- coarse salt

- for serving
- lemon wedges
- pickled okra (optional)

Directions:

1. Supply your smoker with wood pellets and follow the start-up procedure. Preheat the grill, with the lid closed, to 350° F.

2. If using whole wings, cut through the two joints, separating them into drumettes, flats, and wing tips. (Discard the wing tips or save them for chicken stock.) Alternatively, leave the wings whole. Place the chicken in a resealable plastic bag.

3. In a small bowl, make the rub by combining the ingredients. Mix well. Pour the rub over the wings and toss them to thoroughly coat. Refrigerate for 2 hours.

4. In a small bowl, make the Cajun rémoulade by whisking together the mayo, mustard, horseradish, pickle relish, lemon juice, paprika, hot sauce, and Worcestershire. Season with salt to taste. The mixture should be highly seasoned. Transfer to a serving bowl and lightly dust with paprika. Cover and refrigerate until ready to serve.

5. Remove the wings from the refrigerator and allow the excess marinade to drip off. Place the wings on the grate at an angle to the bars. Grill for 20 minutes and then turn. (They'll brown more evenly but will also have less of a tendency to stick.) Continue to cook until the wings are nicely browned and the meat is no longer pink at the bone, about 20 minutes more.

6. Remove the wings from the grill and pile them on a platter. Serve with the Cajun rémoulade, lemon wedges, and pickled okra (if using).

Pulled Pork Loaded Nachos

Servings: 4
Cooking Time: 10 Minutes

Ingredients:

- 2 cups leftover smoked pulled pork
- 1 small sweet onion, diced
- 1 medium tomato, diced
- 1 jalapeño pepper, seeded and diced
- 1 garlic clove, minced
- 1 teaspoon salt
- 1 teaspoon freshly ground black pepper
- 1 bag tortilla chips
- 1 cup shredded Cheddar cheese
- ½ cup The Ultimate BBQ Sauce, divided
- ½ cup shredded jalapeño Monterey Jack cheese
- Juice of ½ lime
- 1 avocado, halved, pitted, and sliced
- 2 tablespoons sour cream
- 1 tablespoon chopped fresh cilantro

Directions:

1. Supply your smoker with wood pellets and follow the start-up procedure. Preheat, with the lid closed, to 375°F.

2. Heat the pulled pork in the microwave.

3. In a medium bowl, combine the onion, tomato, jalapeño, garlic, salt, and pepper, and set aside.

4. Arrange half of the tortilla chips in a large cast iron skillet. Spread half of the warmed pork on top and cover with the Cheddar cheese. Top with half of the onion-jalapeño mixture, then drizzle with ¼ cup of barbecue sauce.

5. Layer on the remaining tortilla chips, then the remaining pork and the Monterey Jack cheese. Top with the remaining onion-jalapeño mixture

and drizzle with the remaining ¼ cup of barbecue sauce.

6. Place the skillet on the grill, close the lid, and smoke for about 10 minutes, or until the cheese is melted and bubbly. (Watch to make sure your chips don't burn!)

7. Squeeze the lime juice over the nachos, top with the avocado slices and sour cream, and garnish with the cilantro before serving hot.

Citrus-infused Marinated Olives

Servings: 6
Cooking Time: 30 Minutes

Ingredients:

- 1½ cups mixed brined olives, with pits
- ½ cup extra virgin olive oil
- 1 tbsp freshly squeezed lemon juice
- 1 garlic clove, peeled and thinly sliced
- 1 tsp smoked Spanish paprika
- 2 sprigs of fresh rosemary
- 2 sprigs of fresh thyme
- 2 bay leaves, fresh or dried
- 1 small dried red chili pepper, deseeded and flesh crumbled, or ¼ tsp crushed red pepper flakes
- 3 strips of orange zest
- 3 strips of lemon zest

Directions:

1. Supply your smoker with wood pellets and follow the start-up procedure. Preheat the grill, with the lid closed, to 180° F.

2. Drain the olives, reserving 1 tablespoon of brine. Spread the olives in a single layer in an aluminum foil roasting pan. Place the pan on the grate and cook the olives for 30 minutes, stirring the olives or shaking the pan once or twice.

3. In a small saucepan on the stovetop over low heat, warm the olive oil. Whisk in the lemon juice and the reserved 1 tablespoon of brine. Stir in the garlic and paprika. Add the rosemary, thyme, bay leaves, chili pepper, and orange and lemon zests. Warm over low heat for 10 minutes. Remove the saucepan from the heat.

4. Transfer the olives and olive oil mixture to a pint jar. Tuck the aromatics around the sides of the jar. Let cool and then cover and refrigerate for up to 5 days. Let the olives come to room temperature before serving.

Chorizo Queso Fundido

Servings: 4-6
Cooking Time: 20 Minutes

Ingredients:

- 1 poblano chile
- 1 cup chopped queso quesadilla or queso Oaxaca
- 1 cup shredded Monterey Jack cheese
- ¼ cup milk
- 1 tablespoon all-purpose flour
- 2 (4-ounce) links Mexican chorizo sausage, casings removed
- ⅓ cup beer
- 1 tablespoon unsalted butter
- 1 small red onion, chopped
- ½ cup whole kernel corn
- 2 serrano chiles or jalapeño peppers, stemmed, seeded, and coarsely chopped
- 1 tablespoon minced garlic
- 1 tablespoon freshly squeezed lime juice
- 1 teaspoon ground cumin
- 1 teaspoon salt
- 1 teaspoon freshly ground black pepper
- 1 tablespoon chopped fresh cilantro
- 1 tablespoon chopped scallions
- Tortilla chips, for serving

Directions:

1. Supply your smoker with wood pellets and follow the start-up procedure. Preheat, with the lid closed, to 350°F.

2. On the smoker or over medium-high heat on the stove top, place the poblano directly on the grate (or burner) to char for 1 to 2 minutes, turning as needed. Remove from heat and place in a closed-up lunch-size paper bag for 2 minutes to sweat and further loosen the skin.

3. Remove the skin and coarsely chop the poblano, removing the seeds; set aside.

4. In a bowl, combine the queso quesadilla, Monterey Jack, milk, and flour; set aside.

5. On the stove top, in a cast iron skillet over medium heat, cook and crumble the chorizo for about 2 minutes.

6. Transfer the cooked chorizo to a small, grill-safe pan and place over indirect heat on the smoker.

7. Place the cast iron skillet on the preheated grill grate. Pour in the beer and simmer for a few minutes, loosening and stirring in any remaining sausage bits from the pan.

8. Add the butter to the pan, then add the cheese mixture a little at a time, stirring constantly.

9. When the cheese is smooth, stir in the onion, corn, serrano chiles, garlic, lime juice, cuvmin, salt, and pepper. Stir in the reserved chopped charred poblano.

10. Close the lid and smoke for 15 to 20 minutes to infuse the queso with smoke flavor and further cook the vegetables.

11. When the cheese is bubbly, top with the chorizo mixture and garnish with the cilantro and scallions.

12. Serve the chorizo queso fundido hot with tortilla chips.

Grilled Guacamole

Servings: 6
Cooking Time: 30 Minutes

Ingredients:

- 3 large avocados, halved and pitted
- 1 lime, halved
- ½ jalapeño, deseeded and deveined
- ½ small white or red onion, peeled
- 2 garlic cloves, peeled and skewered on a toothpick
- 1 tsp coarse salt, plus more
- 1½ tbsp reduced-fat mayo
- 2 tbsp chopped fresh cilantro
- 2 tbsp crumbled queso fresco (optional)
- tortilla chips

Directions:

1. Supply your smoker with wood pellets and follow the start-up procedure. Preheat the grill, with the lid closed, to 225° F.

2. Place the avocados, lime, jalapeño, and onion cut sides down on the grate. Use the toothpicks to balance the garlic cloves between the bars. Smoke for 30 minutes. (You want the vegetables to retain most of their rawness.)

3. Transfer everything to a cutting board. Remove the garlic cloves from the toothpick and roughly chop. Sprinkle with the salt and continue to mince the garlic until it begins to form a paste. Scrape the garlic and salt into a large bowl.

4. Scoop the avocado flesh from the peels into the bowl. Squeeze the juice of ½ lime over the avocado. Mash the avocados but leave them somewhat chunky. Finely dice the jalapeño. Dice 2 tablespoons of onion. (Reserve the remaining

onion for another use.) Add the jalapeño, onion, mayo, and cilantro to the bowl. Stir gently to combine. Taste for seasoning, adding more salt, lime juice, and jalapeño as desired.

5. Transfer the guacamole to a serving bowl. Top with the queso fresco (if using). Serve with tortilla chips.

Pigs In A Blanket

Servings: 4-6
Cooking Time: 15 Minutes

Ingredients:
- 2 Tablespoon Poppy Seeds
- 1 Tablespoon Dried Minced Onion
- 2 Teaspoon garlic, minced
- 2 Tablespoon Sesame Seeds
- 1 Teaspoon salt
- 8 Ounce Original Crescent Dough
- 1/4 Cup Dijon mustard
- 1 Large egg, beaten

Directions:
1. When ready to cook, start your smoker at 350 degrees F, and preheat with lid closed, 10 to 15 minutes.
2. Mix together poppy seeds, dried minced onion, dried minced garlic, salt and sesame seeds. Set aside.
3. Cut each triangle of crescent roll dough into thirds lengthwise, making 3 small strips from each roll.
4. Brush the dough strips lightly with Dijon mustard. Put the mini hot dogs on 1 end of the dough and roll up.
5. Arrange them, seam side down, on a greased baking pan. Brush with egg wash and sprinkle with seasoning mixture.

6. Bake in smoker until golden brown, about 12 to 15 minutes.
7. Serve with mustard or dipping sauce of your choice. Enjoy!

Simple Cream Cheese Sausage Balls

Servings: 5
Cooking Time: 30 Minutes

Ingredients:
- 1 pound ground hot sausage, uncooked
- 8 ounces cream cheese, softened
- 1 package mini filo dough shells

Directions:
1. Supply your smoker with wood pellets and follow the start-up procedure. Preheat, with the lid closed, to 350°F.
2. In a large bowl, using your hands, thoroughly mix together the sausage and cream cheese until well blended.
3. Place the filo dough shells on a rimmed perforated pizza pan or into a mini muffin tin.
4. Roll the sausage and cheese mixture into 1-inch balls and place into the filo shells.
5. Place the pizza pan or mini muffin tin on the grill, close the lid, and smoke the sausage balls for 30 minutes, or until cooked through and the sausage is no longer pink.
6. Plate and serve warm.

Deviled Eggs With Smoked Paprika

Servings: 6
Cooking Time: 30 Minutes

Ingredients:

- 6 large eggs
- 3 tbsp reduced-fat mayo, plus more
- 1 tsp Dijon or yellow mustard
- ½ tsp Spanish smoked paprika or regular paprika, plus more
- dash of hot sauce
- coarse salt
- freshly ground black pepper
- for garnishing
- small sprigs of fresh parsley, dill, tarragon, or cilantro
- chopped chives
- minced scallions
- Mustard Caviar
- sliced green or black olives
- celery leaves
- sliced radishes
- diced bell peppers
- sliced cherry tomatoes
- fresh or pickled jalapeños
- sliced or diced pickles
- slivers of sun-dried tomatoes
- bacon crumbles
- smoked salmon
- Hawaiian black salt
- Caviar

Directions:

1. Supply your smoker with wood pellets and follow the start-up procedure. Preheat the grill, with the lid closed, to 180° F.

2. On the stovetop over medium-high heat, bring a saucepan of water to a boil. (Make sure there's enough water in the saucepan to cover the eggs by 1 inch [5cm].) Use a slotted spoon to gently lower the eggs into the water. Lower the heat to maintain a simmer. Set a timer for 13 minutes.

3. Prepare an ice bath by combining ice and cold water in a large bowl. Carefully transfer the eggs to the ice bath when the timer goes off.

4. When the eggs are cool enough to handle, gently tap them all over to crack the shell. Carefully peel the eggs. Rinse under cold running water to remove any clinging bits of shell, but don't dry the eggs. (A damp surface will help the smoke adhere to the egg whites.)

5. Place the eggs on the grate and smoke until the eggs take on a light brown patina from the smoke, about 25 minutes. Transfer the eggs to a cutting board, handling them as little as possible.

6. Slice each egg in half lengthwise with a sharp knife. Wipe any yolk off the blade before slicing the next egg. Gently remove the yolks and place them in a food processor. Pulse to break up the yolks. Add the mayo, mustard, paprika, and hot sauce. Season with salt and pepper to taste. Pulse until the filling is smooth. Add additional mayo 1 teaspoon at a time if the mixture is a little dry. (It shouldn't be too loose either.)

7. Spoon the filling into each egg half or pipe it in using a small resealable plastic bag. You can also use a pastry bag fitted with a fluted tip.

8. Place the eggs on a platter and lightly dust with paprika. Accompany with one or more of the suggested garnishes.

Smoked Cashews

Servings: 6

Cooking Time: 60 Minutes

Ingredients:

- 1 pound roasted, salted cashews

Directions:

1. Supply your smoker with wood pellets and follow the start-up procedure. Preheat the grill, with the lid closed, to 120°F.

2. Pour the cashews onto a rimmed baking sheet and smoke for 1 hour, stirring once about halfway through the smoking time.

3. Remove the cashews from the grill, let cool, and store in an airtight container for as long as you can resist.

Pig Pops (sweet-hot Bacon On A Stick)

Servings: 24

Cooking Time: 30 Minutes

Ingredients:

- Nonstick cooking spray, oil, or butter, for greasing
- 2 pounds thick-cut bacon (24 slices)
- 24 metal skewers
- 1 cup packed light brown sugar
- 2 to 3 teaspoons cayenne pepper
- ½ cup maple syrup, divided

Directions:

1. Supply your smoker with wood pellets and follow the start-up procedure. Preheat, with the lid closed, to 350°F.

2. Coat a disposable aluminum foil baking sheet with cooking spray, oil, or butter.

3. Thread each bacon slice onto a metal skewer and place on the prepared baking sheet.

4. In a medium bowl, stir together the brown sugar and cayenne.

5. Baste the top sides of the bacon with ¼ cup of maple syrup.

6. Sprinkle half of the brown sugar mixture over the bacon.

7. Place the baking sheet on the grill, close the lid, and smoke for 15 to 30 minutes.

8. Using tongs, flip the bacon skewers. Baste with the remaining ¼ cup of maple syrup and top with the remaining brown sugar mixture.

9. Continue smoking with the lid closed for 10 to 15 minutes, or until crispy. You can eyeball the bacon and smoke to your desired doneness, but the actual ideal internal temperature for bacon is 155°F

10. Using tongs, carefully remove the bacon skewers from the grill. Let cool completely before handling.

Chuckwagon Beef Jerky

Servings: 6

Cooking Time: 300 Minutes

Ingredients:

- 2½lb (1.2kg) boneless top or bottom round steak, sirloin tip, flank steak, or venison
- 1 cup sugar-free dark-colored soda
- 1 cup cold brewed coffee
- ½ cup light soy sauce
- ¼ cup Worcestershire sauce
- 2 tbsp whiskey (optional)
- 2 tsp chili powder
- 1½ tsp garlic salt
- 1 tsp onion powder
- 1 tsp pink curing salt

Directions:

1. Slice the meat into ¼-inch-thick (.5cm) strips, trimming off any visible fat or gristle. (Slice against the grain for more tender jerky and with the grain for chewier jerky.) Place the meat in a large resealable plastic bag.

2. In a small bowl, whisk together the soda, coffee, soy sauce, Worcestershire sauce, whiskey (if using), chili powder, garlic salt, onion powder, and curing salt (if using). Whisk until the salt dissolves. Pour the mixture over the meat and reseal the bag. Refrigerate for 24 to 48 hours, turning the bag several times to redistribute the brine.

3. Supply your smoker with wood pellets and follow the start-up procedure. Preheat the grill, with the lid closed, to 150° F.

4. Drain the meat and discard the brine. Place the strips of meat in a single layer on paper towels and blot any excess moisture.

5. Place the meat in a single layer on the grate and smoke for 4 to 5 hours, turning once or twice. (If you're aware of hot spots on your grate, rotate the strips so they smoke evenly.) To test for doneness, bend one or two pieces in the middle. They should be dry but still somewhat pliant. Or simply eat a piece to see if it's done to your liking.

6. For the best texture, when you remove the meat from the grill, place the still-warm jerky in a resealable plastic bag and let rest for 30 minutes. (You might see condensation form on the inside of the bag, but the moisture will be reabsorbed by the meat.) Or let the meat cool completely and then store in a resealable plastic bag or covered container. The jerky will last a few days at room temperature but will last longer (up to 2 weeks) if refrigerated.

Smoked Cheese

Servings: 4
Cooking Time: 150 Minutes

Ingredients:

- 1 (2-pound) block medium Cheddar cheese, or your favorite cheese, quartered lengthwise

Directions:

1. Supply your smoker with wood pellets and follow the start-up procedure. Preheat the grill, with the lid closed, to 90°F.

2. Place the cheese directly on the grill grate and smoke for 2 hours, 30 minutes, checking frequently to be sure it's not melting. If the cheese begins to melt, try flipping it. If that doesn't help, remove it from the grill and refrigerate for about 1 hour and then return it to the cold smoker.

3. Remove the cheese, place it in a zip-top bag, and refrigerate overnight.

4. Slice the cheese and serve with crackers, or grate it and use for making a smoked mac and cheese.

Roasted Red Pepper Dip

Servings: 8
Cooking Time: 45 Minutes

Ingredients:

- 4 red bell peppers, halved, destemmed, and deseeded
- 1 cup English walnuts, divided
- 1 small white onion, peeled and coarsely chopped
- 2 garlic cloves, peeled and smashed with a chef's knife
- ¼ cup extra virgin olive oil, plus more
- 1 tbsp balsamic vinegar or balsamic glaze
- 1 tsp honey (eliminate if using balsamic glaze)

- 1 tsp coarse salt, plus more
- 1 tsp ground cumin
- 1 tsp smoked paprika
- ½ to 1 tsp Aleppo red pepper flakes, plus more
- ¼ cup fresh white breadcrumbs (optional)
- distilled water (optional)
- assorted crudités or wedges of pita bread

Directions:

1. Supply your smoker with wood pellets and follow the start-up procedure. Preheat the grill, with the lid closed, to 400° F.

2. Place the peppers skin side down on the grate and grill until the skins blister and the flesh softens, about 30 minutes. Transfer the peppers to a bowl and cover with plastic wrap. Let cool to room temperature. Remove the skins with a paring knife or your fingers. Coarsely chop or tear the peppers.

3. Place ¾ cup of walnuts in an aluminum foil roasting pan. Place the pan on the grate and toast for 10 to 15 minutes, stirring twice. Remove the pan from the grill and let the walnuts cool.

4. Place the peppers, onion, garlic, and walnuts in a food processor fitted with the chopping blade. Pulse several times. Add the olive oil, balsamic vinegar, honey, salt, cumin, paprika, and red pepper flakes. Process until the mixture is fairly smooth. Taste for seasoning, adding more salt or red pepper flakes (if desired). (If the mixture is too loose, add breadcrumbs until the texture is to your liking. If it's too thick, add olive oil or water 1 tablespoon at a time.)

5. Transfer the dip to a serving bowl. Use the back of a spoon to make a shallow depression in the center. Top with the remaining ¼ cup of walnuts and drizzle olive oil in the depression. Serve with crudités or pita bread.

Delicious Deviled Crab Appetizer

Servings: 30
Cooking Time: 10 Minutes

Ingredients:

- Nonstick cooking spray, oil, or butter, for greasing
- 1 cup panko breadcrumbs, divided
- 1 cup canned corn, drained
- ½ cup chopped scallions, divided
- ½ red bell pepper, finely chopped
- 16 ounces jumbo lump crabmeat
- ¾ cup mayonnaise, divided
- 1 egg, beaten
- 1 teaspoon salt
- 1 teaspoon freshly ground black pepper
- 2 teaspoons cayenne pepper, divided
- Juice of 1 lemon

Directions:

1. Supply your smoker with wood pellets and follow the start-up procedure. Preheat, with the lid closed, to 425°F.

2. Spray three 12-cup mini muffin pans with cooking spray and divide ½ cup of the panko between 30 of the muffin cups, pressing into the bottoms and up the sides. (Work in batches, if necessary, depending on the number of pans you have.)

3. In a medium bowl, combine the corn, ¼ cup of scallions, the bell pepper, crabmeat, half of the mayonnaise, the egg, salt, pepper, and 1 teaspoon of cayenne pepper.

4. Gently fold in the remaining ½ cup of breadcrumbs and divide the mixture between the prepared mini muffin cups.

5. Place the pans on the grill grate, close the lid, and smoke for 10 minutes, or until golden brown.

6. In a small bowl, combine the lemon juice and the remaining mayonnaise, scallions, and cayenne pepper to make a sauce.

7. Brush the tops of the mini crab cakes with the sauce and serve hot.

Smoked Turkey Sandwich

Servings: 1
Cooking Time: 15 Minutes

Ingredients:
- 2 slices sourdough bread
- 2 tablespoons butter, at room temperature
- 2 (1-ounce) slices Swiss cheese
- 4 ounces leftover Smoked Turkey
- 1 teaspoon garlic salt

Directions:

1. Supply your smoker with wood pellets and follow the start-up procedure. Preheat the grill, with the lid closed, to 375°F.

2. Coat one side of each bread slice with 1 tablespoon of butter and sprinkle the buttered sides with garlic salt.

3. Place 1 slice of cheese on each unbuttered side of the bread, and then put the turkey on the cheese.

4. Close the sandwich, buttered sides out, and place it directly on the grill grate. Cook for 5 minutes. Flip the sandwich and cook for 5 minutes more. Remove the sandwich from the grill, cut it in half, and serve.

Sriracha & Maple Cashews

Servings: 10
Cooking Time: 60 Minutes

Ingredients:
- 2 tbsp unsalted butter
- 3 tbsp pure maple syrup
- 1 tbsp sriracha
- 1 tsp coarse salt (use only if nuts are unsalted)
- 2½ cups unsalted cashews

Directions:

1. Supply your smoker with wood pellets and follow the start-up procedure. Preheat the grill, with the lid closed, to 250° F.

2. In a small saucepan on the stovetop over low heat, melt the butter. Add the maple syrup, sriracha, and salt (if using). Stir until combined. Add the nuts and stir gently to coat thoroughly.

3. Spread the nuts in a single layer in an aluminum foil roasting pan coated with cooking spray. Place the pan on the grate and smoke the nuts until they're lightly toasted, about 1 hour, stirring once or twice.

4. Remove the pan from the grill and let the nuts cool for 15 minutes. They'll be sticky at first but will crisp up. Break them up with your fingers and store at room temperature in an airtight container, such as a lidded glass jar.

Jalapeño Poppers With Chipotle Sour Cream

Servings: 8
Cooking Time: 45 Minutes

Ingredients:
- 3 strips of thin-sliced bacon
- 12 large jalapeños, red, green, or a mix
- 8oz (225g) light cream cheese, at room temperature
- 1 cup shredded pepper Jack, Monterey Jack, or Cheddar cheese
- 1 tsp chili powder
- ½ tsp garlic salt

- smoked paprika
- for the sour cream
- 1¼ cups light sour cream
- juice of ½ lime
- ½ to 1 canned chipotle peppers in adobo sauce, finely minced, plus 1 tsp of sauce, plus more
- 1 tbsp minced fresh cilantro leaves
- ½ tsp coarse salt, plus more

Directions:

1. Supply your smoker with wood pellets and follow the start-up procedure. Preheat the grill, with the lid closed, to 375° F.

2. Line a rimmed sheet pan with aluminum foil and place a wire rack on top. Place the bacon in a single layer on the wire rack. Place the pan on the grate and grill until the bacon is crisp and golden brown, about 20 minutes. Transfer the bacon to paper towels to cool and then crumble. Set aside.

3. In a small bowl, make the chipotle sour cream by whisking together the ingredients. Add more salt, chipotle peppers, or adobe sauce to taste. Cover and refrigerate.

4. Slice the jalapeños lengthwise through their stems. Scrape out the veins and seeds with the edge of a small metal spoon.

5. In a small bowl, beat together the cream cheese, shredded cheese, chili powder, and garlic salt. Stir in the crumbled bacon. Mound the cream cheese mixture in the jalapeño halves. Line another rimmed sheet pan with aluminum foil and place a wire rack on top. Place the jalapeños filled side up in a single layer on the wire rack.

6. Place the sheet pan on the grate and roast the jalapeños until the filling has melted and the peppers have softened, about 20 to 25 minutes. (They should no longer look bright in color.)

Remove the pan from the grill and let the peppers rest for 5 minutes.

7. Transfer the poppers to a platter and lightly dust with paprika. Serve with the chipotle sour cream.

Cold-smoked Cheese

Servings: 6
Cooking Time: 180 Minutes

Ingredients:

- 2lb (1kg) well-chilled hard or semi-hard cheese, such as:
- Edam
- Gouda
- Cheddar
- Monterey Jack
- pepper Jack
- goat cheese
- fresh mozzarella
- Muenster
- aged Parmigiano-Reggiano
- Gruyère
- blue cheese

Directions:

1. Unwrap the cheese and remove any protective wax or coating. Cut into 4-ounce (110g) portions to increase the surface area.

2. If possible, move your smoker to a shady area. Place 1 resealable plastic bag filled with ice on top of the drip pan. This is especially important on a warm day because you want to keep the interior temperature of the grill between 70 and 90°F (21 and 32°C) or below.

3. Place a grill mat on one side of the grate. Place the cheese on the mat and allow space between each piece.

4. Fill your smoking tube or pellet maze (see Cast Iron Skillets and Grill Pans) with pellets or sawdust and light according to the manufacturer's instructions. Place the smoking tube on the grate near—but not on—the grill mat. When the tube is smoking consistently, close the grill lid.

5. Smoke the cheese for 1 to 3 hours, replacing the pellets or sawdust and ice if necessary. Monitor the temperature and make sure the cheese isn't beginning to melt. Carefully lift the mat with the cheese to a rimmed baking sheet and let the cheese cool completely before handling.

6. Package the smoked cheese in cheese storage paper or bags or vacuum-seal the cheese, labeling each. (While you can wrap the cheese tightly in plastic wrap, the cheese will spoil faster.) Let the cheese rest for at least 2 to 3 days before eating. It will be even better after 2 weeks.

POULTRY RECIPES

Crispy Chicken Quarters

Servings: 4
Cooking Time: 55 Minutes

Ingredients:
- 2 Cups Alabama White Sauce
- 1 Tbsp Champion Chicken
- 4 Chicken Leg Quarters
- 1 Tbsp Olive Oil

Directions:

1. Place chicken leg quarters on a sheet tray lined with aluminum foil. Gently pull away the skin from the chicken leg quarters, then drizzle inside and out with olive oil. Season the chicken leg quarters all over and under the skin with Champion Chicken. Let chicken sit out at room temperature for 1 hour.

2. Supply your smoker with wood pellets and follow the start-up procedure. Preheat the grill, with the lid open, to 450° F. If using a gas or charcoal grill, set it up for medium-high heat and direct heat.

3. Sear the leg quarters on all sides over direct flame until crispy and golden brown. Transfer to indirect heat and close the sear slide. Reduce temperature to 350° F and grill the chicken for 45 minutes, turning occasionally, until chicken registers an internal temperature of 165° F.

4. Remove chicken from grill and allow to rest for 10 minutes. Serve chicken hot with a generous drizzling of Alabama white sauce*.

Grilled Cheesy Chicken

Servings: 4
Cooking Time: 45 Minutes

Ingredients:
- 4 Aged Chedder Cheese, Sliced
- 32 Oz Chicken Broth
- 1 Tsp Extra-Virgin Olive Oil
- Sweet Heat Rub And Grill
- 4 Plump Chicken, Boneless/Skinless

Directions:

1. Supply your smoker with wood pellets and follow the start-up procedure. Preheat the grill, with the lid open, to 350° F.

2. Remove the chicken from the brine. Pat the breasts dry and lightly brush olive oil on both sides of the chicken. Take your knife and slice diagonally across the top of each breast. Sprinkle a lit amount of Sweet Heat Rub and Grill on each side.

3. Barbecue your chicken breasts for 30 minutes. Next, place a slice of cheddar cheese on top of each breast.

4. Heat for another 5-10 minutes or until the cheese has fully melted into the incisions you made earlier. Remove and serve for a tender chicken breast with a spicy kick and hot cheesy center. You'll receive too much credit for a recipe this easy.

Texas Style Black Pepper Turkey

Servings: 6
Cooking Time: 240 Minutes

Ingredients:
- 1/2 Cup Coarse Black Pepper
- 1Lb Butter
- 1/2 Cup Salt, Kosher
- 1 Brined Turkey

Directions:

1. Supply your smoker with wood pellets and follow the start-up procedure. Preheat the grill, with the lid closed, to 300° F.

2. Liberally season Turkey with equal parts kosher salt and coarse black pepper.

3. Cook on grill until Internal temp reaches approximately 145°F or the skin has darkened to your liking.

4. Place turkey in a roasting pan topped with a pound of chopped butter and cover.

5. Return to the grill until internal temp of the thigh and breast reaches 165°F

6. Let rest for 30 minutes, carve and serve.

Lemon Cajun Chicken Carbonara

Servings: 2
Cooking Time: 20 Minutes

Ingredients:

- 2 Slices Thick-Cut Bacon
- 1 Tbsp Cajun Seasoning
- 8 Oz. Chicken Breast
- 4 Egg, Yolk
- 1 Tbsp Garlic Clove, Minced
- 1 ¼ Cup Heavy Cream
- 2 Tbsp + 1 Tbsp Divided Italian Parsley
- 1 ½ Tbsp Divided Olive Oil
- ½ Cup Grated Parmesan Cheese
- ½ Tbsp Hickory Bacon Seasoning
- ¼ Tbsp Red Chili Flakes
- 1 Tbsp Scallions
- ½ Lb. Spaghetti

Directions:

1. Supply your smoker with wood pellets and follow the start-up procedure. Preheat the grill, with the lid open, to 400° F. If using a gas or charcoal grill, set the temp to medium-high heat.

In a medium bowl, combine chicken, Hickory Bacon Seasoning, Cajun seasoning, and ½ tablespoon of olive oil. Toss to combine. Set aside or place in a bag and marinate in the refrigerator for 30 minutes to 1 hour.

2. Place tenders on preheated grill and cook for 3 minutes per side. Remove from grill and place on a cutting board to rest for 5 minutes. Slice thinly on the diagonal and set aside.

3. In a large stock pot, boil pasta per package instructions. Drain and set aside.

4. In a large skillet heat 1 tablespoon of oil over medium heat. Sauté bacon, stirring frequently, for 3 minutes or until crisp. Add garlic and cook for one minute. Lower heat to low and add in drained pasta. Using tongs, gently toss pasta to coat in oil and bacon.

5. In a mixing bowl, whisk together heavy cream, parmesan, egg yolks, and 2 tablespoons of parsley. Slowly pour over pasta, continuously stirring, as to not scramble eggs. After 2 minutes, the sauce will thicken. Add in chicken and lemon zest, and gently stir another minute. Transfer to serving dishes and garnish with additional parsley and red chili flakes.

Roasted Buffalo Wings

Servings: 4
Cooking Time: 30 Minutes

Ingredients:

- 4 Pound chicken wings
- 1 Tablespoon corn starch
- Chicken Rub
- kosher salt
- 1/2 Cup Frank's RedHot Sauce
- 1/4 Cup spicy mustard
- 6 Tablespoon unsalted butter

Directions:

1. Supply your smoker with wood pellets and follow the start-up procedure. Preheat the grill, with the lid closed, to 375° F.

2. While grill is preheating, dry off chicken wings with a paper towel. Place wings in a large bowl and sprinkle with cornstarch, Traeger Chicken Rub and salt to taste. Mix to coat both sides of the chicken wings.

3. When the grill is hot, place the wings on the grill and cook for 35 minutes total, turning halfway through cook time. Grill: 375 ˚F

4. Check the internal temperature of the wings at 35 minutes. The internal temperature should be at least 165˚F. However, an internal temperature of 175-180˚F will yield a better texture. Grill: 375 ˚F Probe: 175 ˚F

5. For the Buffalo Sauce: In a saucepot, add the Franks Red Hot, mustard and butter. Whisk to combine and heat through on the stove top. Keep sauce warm while the wings are cooking.

6. When wings are done, remove from grill and place into a medium bowl Pour the buffalo sauce over the wings, turning with tongs to coat. Grill: 375 ˚F

7. Cook for an additional 10-15 minutes on the grill for the sauce to set. Serve wings with ranch or blue cheese dressing. Enjoy!

Smoked Turkey Wings

Servings: 2
Cooking Time: 60 Minutes

Ingredients:
- 4 turkey wings
- 1 batch Sweet and Spicy Cinnamon Rub

Directions:

1. Supply your smoker with wood pellets and follow the start-up procedure. Preheat the grill, with the lid closed, to 180°F.

2. Using your hands, work the rub into the turkey wings, coating them completely.

3. Place the wings directly on the grill grate and cook for 30 minutes.

4. Increase the grill's temperature to 325°F and continue to cook until the turkey's internal temperature reaches 170°F. Remove the wings from the grill and serve immediately.

Cider-brined Turkey

Servings: 8
Cooking Time: 180 Minutes

Ingredients:
- 1 whole turkey, about 12 to 14lb (4.5 to 5.4kg), thawed if frozen
- 1 white onion, peeled and sliced into quarters
- 1 apple, cut into wedges
- 2 celery stalks, sliced into 2-inch (5cm) pieces
- sprigs of fresh sage, rosemary, parsley, or thyme
- 8 tbsp unsalted butter, at room temperature
- coarse salt
- freshly ground black pepper
- for the brine
- 1 quart (1 liter) apple cider or apple juice
- 3 quarts (3 liters) cold distilled water
- ¾ cup coarse salt
- ½ cup light brown sugar or low-carb substitute
- 3 garlic cloves, peeled and smashed with a chef's knife
- 3 bay leaves

Directions:

1. In a large food-safe bucket, make the brine by combining the apple cider, water, salt, and brown sugar. Stir until the salt and sugar dissolve. Add the garlic and bay leaves. Submerge the turkey in the brine. If it floats, place a resealable bag of ice on top. Refrigerate for at least 8 hours and up to 16 hours.

2. Supply your smoker with wood pellets and follow the start-up procedure. Preheat the grill, with the lid closed, to 350° F.

3. Remove the turkey from the brine and pat dry with paper towels. Discard the brine. Place the onion, apple, celery, and herbs in the main cavity. Tie the legs together with butcher's twine. Fold the wings behind the back. Rub the outside with butter. Lightly season with salt and pepper.

4. Place the turkey breast side up on a wire rack in a shallow roasting pan. Place the pan on the grate and roast the turkey until the internal temperature in the thickest part of a thigh reaches 165°F (74°C), about 2½ to 3 hours.

5. Transfer the turkey to a cutting board and let rest for 20 minutes. (Save the drippings to make from-scratch turkey gravy.) Carve the turkey and arrange the meat on a large platter before serving.

Bbq Chicken Wings With Spicy Honey Glaze

Servings: 4
Cooking Time: 30 Minutes

Ingredients:

- 4 Pound chicken wings
- 6 Ounce Chicken Rub
- 2 Tablespoon corn starch
- 1 Cup honey
- 1 Cup Sriracha
- 1/2 Cup soy sauce
- 2 Tablespoon sesame oil
- 3 Tablespoon unsalted butter
- 2 Tablespoon sesame seeds

Directions:

1. Supply your smoker with wood pellets and follow the start-up procedure. Preheat the grill, with the lid closed, to 375° F.

2. While grill is preheating, dry off chicken wings with a paper towel. Mix the Traeger Chicken rub with the cornstarch and coat both sides of the chicken wings.

3. When the grill is heated, place the wings on the grill for 35 minutes flipping half way through. Grill: 375 °F

4. While the wings are cooking, mix the honey, Sriracha, soy sauce, sesame seed oil, and unsalted butter and heat on a stove top.

5. After the wings have cooked for 35 minutes, check the temperature. The minimum temperature must reach an internal temperature of 165 degrees F. An internal temperature between 175 to 180 degrees F may yield a better texture. Grill: 375 °F Probe: 177 °F

6. When wings are done, place in large bowl and toss with the warmed sauce.

7. Place wings on platter and sprinkle the sesame seeds. Enjoy!

Skinny Smoked Chicken Breasts

Servings: 4-6
Cooking Time: 85 Minutes

Ingredients:

- 2½ pounds boneless, skinless chicken breasts
- Salt
- Freshly ground black pepper

Directions:

1. Supply your smoker with wood pellets and follow the start-up procedure. Preheat the grill, with the lid closed, to 180°F.

2. Season the chicken breasts all over with salt and pepper.

3. Place the breasts directly on the grill grate and smoke for 1 hour.

4. Increase the grill's temperature to 325°F and continue to cook until the chicken's internal temperature reaches 170°F. Remove the breasts from the grill and serve immediately.

Peanut Butter Chicken Wings

Servings: 4

Cooking Time: 35 Minutes

Ingredients:

- 1 Tsp Black Peppercorns, Ground
- 2 Tbsp Brown Sugar
- 4 Lbs Chicken Wings, Trimmed And Patted Dry
- 2 Tbsp Honey
- 1/4 Cup Peanut Butter
- 10 Oz Peanuts, Whole
- 2 Tsp Sweet Rib Rub
- 1/2 Red Onion, Minced
- 1/2 Cup Strawberry Preserves
- 1 Tbsp Thai Chili Sauce
- 1/4 Cup Worcestershire Sauce

Directions:

1. Place chicken wings in a 9 x13 glass baking dish. Pour mixture over chicken, cover with plastic wrap, and refrigerate for 2 hours.

2. Supply your smoker with wood pellets and follow the start-up procedure. Preheat the grill, with the lid open, to 400° F. Preheat griddle to medium-low flame. If using a gas or charcoal grill, set it to medium-high heat.

3. Place wings directly on grill grate, over indirect heat, and cook for 20 to 25 minutes, rotating wings every 5 minutes.

4. Meanwhile, place shelled peanuts on the griddle, turning occasionally with a metal spatula for 5 to 7 minutes, to lightly roast. Remove from the griddle and set aside to cool.

5. Remove wings from grill and allow to rest for 5 minutes. While wings are resting, shell the peanuts, and transfer to a resealable plastic bag. Use a rolling pin to crush the peanuts, then scatter peanuts on top of the chicken wings. Serve warm.

Smoked Turkey Jerky

Servings: 6

Cooking Time: 240 Minutes

Ingredients:

- 1/2 Cup soy sauce
- 1/4 Cup water
- 2 Tablespoon honey
- 2 Tablespoon Asian chili garlic sauce
- 2 Tablespoon lime juice
- 1 Tablespoon Morton Tender Quick Home Meat Cure
- 2 Pound (4-5 lb) boneless turkey breast

Directions:

1. In a mixing bowl, combine the soy sauce, water, honey, chili-garlic paste, lime juice, and curing salt, if using. With a sharp knife, slice the turkey into 1/4" thick slices with the grain, which helps it hold together better as it dries. (This is easier if the meat is partially frozen.) Trim any fat, membrane, or connective tissue.

2. Put the turkey slices in a large resealable plastic bag. Pour the marinade mixture over the turkey, and massage the bag so that all the slices

get coated with the marinade. Seal the bag and refrigerate for several hours, or overnight.

3. Supply your smoker with wood pellets and follow the start-up procedure. Preheat the grill, with the lid closed, to 180° F.

4. Remove the turkey from the marinade and discard the marinade. Dry the turkey slices between paper towels. Arrange in a single layer directly on the grill grate.

5. Smoke for 2 to 4 hours, or until the jerky is dry but still chewy and somewhat pliant when you bend a piece. Grill: 180 °F

6. Transfer to a resealable plastic bag while the jerky's still warm. Let the jerky rest for an hour at room temperature. Squeeze any air from the bag, and refrigerate the jerky. It will keep for several weeks. Enjoy!

Smoked Maple Syrup Thanksgiving Turkey

Servings: 8
Cooking Time: 375 Minutes

Ingredients:
- 1 Cup Butter, Room Temp
- 1/2 Cup Maple Syrup
- 2 Tablespoons Champion Chicken Seasoning
- 1, (Pre-Brined) Turkey, Whole

Directions:

1. Supply your smoker with wood pellets and follow the start-up procedure. Preheat the grill, with the lid closed, to 250° F.

2. Combine the melted butter and maple syrup in a bowl. With the Marinade Injector, fill with the butter and syrup mixture and pierce the meat with the needle while pushing on the plunger, injecting the flavor. You want to inject the marinade into the thickest part of the breast, thigh, and wings.

3. Next, combine the room temperature butter and Champion Chicken seasoning and spread all over the turkey, making sure that you get it under the skin as well.

4. Place the turkey in an aluminum pan to catch all the drippings (this makes incredible gravy) and place on the grill.

5. When the breast and thigh meat of the turkey reaches 165°F to 170°F, remove from grill and let rest 15 minutes before carving. Happy Thanksgiving!

Fried Chicken Sliders

Servings: 8
Cooking Time: 30 Minutes

Ingredients:
- 8 Slider Buns
- ½ Cup Buttermilk
- 4 Horizontally Cut Chicken Breasts
- 2 Cups Flour, All-Purpose
- 1 Tablespoon Hot Sauce
- ¼ Cup Mayonnaise
- 2 Quarts Cooking Canola Or Soybean Oil
- ½ Cup Spicy Bread And Butter Pickle Slices
- ½ Tablespoon Champion Chicken Seasoning

Directions:

1. Supply your smoker with wood pellets and follow the start-up procedure. Preheat the grill, with the lid open, to 350° F. If you're using a gas or charcoal grill, set it up for medium heat.

2. Place a deep cast iron pan on the grill and fill it with about 3 inches of cooking oil. Place a temperature probe into the oil.

3. While the oil heats, combine the buttermilk, hot sauce and Champion Chicken seasoning in a

resealable plastic bag. Seal and shake to mix, then place the chicken in the bag and turn to coat.

4. Place the flour on a plate and dip the chicken in the flour to coat. Place the chicken on a wire rack set on a baking sheet and allow the coated chicken to set for 10 minutes, then dip again in the flour.

5. Once the oil in the cast iron pan reaches 350°F, place a temperature probe in a piece of chicken and fry the chicken, 2-3 pieces at a time. The oil temperature in the pan will drop by 25-30 degrees, so make sure not to put more than 3 pieces of chicken in the pan or your chicken will be greasy.

6. Fry the chicken until golden brown, crispy, and the internal temperature of the chicken is 170°F. Remove the chicken and place on a plate lined with paper towels. Allow the chicken to drain and rest for 5 minutes. Fry the remaining chicken pieces, reinserting the temperature probe.

7. Once the chicken is all fried, place the chicken on the slider buns, top with spicy bread and butter pickles, and a swoop of mayo, serve immediately.

Wild West Wings

Servings: 4
Cooking Time: 60 Minutes

Ingredients:
- 2 pounds chicken wings
- 2 tablespoons extra-virgin olive oil
- 2 packages ranch dressing mix (such as Hidden Valley brand)
- ¼ cup prepared ranch dressing (optional)

Directions:

1. Supply your smoker with wood pellets and follow the start-up procedure. Preheat, with the lid closed, to 350°F.

2. Place the chicken wings in a large bowl and toss with the olive oil and ranch dressing mix.

3. Arrange the wings directly on the grill, or line the grill with aluminum foil for easy cleanup, close the lid, and smoke for 25 minutes.

4. Flip and smoke for 20 to 35 minutes more, or until a meat thermometer inserted in the thickest part of the wings reads 165°F and the wings are crispy. (Note: The wings will likely be done after 45 minutes, but an extra 10 to 15 minutes makes them crispy without drying the meat.)

5. Serve warm with ranch dressing (if using).

Spatchcocked Chicken With White Barbecue Sauce

Servings: 4
Cooking Time: 60 Minutes

Ingredients:
- 1 whole chicken, about 4 to 4½lb (1.8 to 2kg), preferably organic or farm raised
- extra virgin olive oil
- White Barbecue Sauce
- chopped fresh chives (optional)
- for the brine
- ½ gallon (1.9 liters) distilled water
- ½ cup kosher salt
- 2 tbsp light brown sugar or low-carb substitute
- for the rub
- ¼ cup coarse salt
- ¼ cup granulated light brown sugar or low-carb substitute
- ¼ cup sweet or smoked paprika
- 2 tbsp freshly ground black pepper

- 1 tbsp granulated garlic
- 2 tsp dried thyme
- ½ tsp ground cayenne

Directions:

1. In a large stockpot on the stovetop over medium-high heat, make the brine by combining the ingredients. Bring the mixture to a boil. Stir until the salt and sugar dissolve. Remove the pot from the stovetop and let the brine cool to room temperature. Cover and refrigerate until cool.

2. Remove the backbone of the chicken by using a sharp knife, starting at the tail and cutting through the rib bones. Repeat on the other side of the backbone. Fold the two halves backward to release the cartilaginous breastbone. (You might have to use a knife to slice through the thin skin on either side.) Remove the breastbone. Turn the chicken over and gently flatten it with the palm of your hand. Submerge the chicken in the brine. If it floats, place a resealable bag of ice on top. Refrigerate for 4 to 6 hours.

3. Supply your smoker with wood pellets and follow the start-up procedure. Preheat the grill, with the lid closed, to 325° F.

4. In a small bowl, make the rub by combining the ingredients.

5. Rinse the chicken with cold running water and dry with paper towels. (Discard the brine.) Coat the skin with olive oil. Lightly dust the chicken on both sides with the rub. (Save the remainder for another grill session.) Tuck the wingtips behind the chicken's back.

6. Place the chicken ribs side down on the grate and grill until the skin is nicely browned and the internal temperature in a thigh reaches 170°F (77°C), about 1 hour.

7. Transfer the chicken to a platter. Spoon the white barbecue sauce over the chicken. Spread the sauce with a basting brush, letting it pool in places. Lightly scatter the chives over the top. Carve the chicken and serve with extra sauce on the side.

County Fair Turkey Legs

Servings: 4
Cooking Time: 90 Minutes

Ingredients:
- 4 turkey legs, each about 1lb (450g)
- for the brine
- ½ gallon (1.9 liters) distilled water
- ½ cup kosher salt
- ¼ cup light brown sugar or low-carb substitute
- 2½ tsp pink curing salt #1
- 1 tsp liquid smoke (optional)

Directions:

1. In a stockpot on the stovetop over medium-high heat, make the brine by combining the ingredients. Bring the mixture to a boil. Stir until the salts and sugar dissolve. Remove the pot from the stovetop and let the brine cool to room temperature. Cover and refrigerate until cool.

2. Submerge the turkey legs in the brine. If they float, place a resealable bag of ice on top. Refrigerate for 24 hours, turning from time to time so the legs cure evenly.

3. Supply your smoker with wood pellets and follow the start-up procedure. Preheat the grill, with the lid closed, to 325° F.

4. Remove the turkey legs from the brine and discard the liquid. Rinse the legs under cold running water and pat dry with paper towels.

5. Place the turkey legs on the grate and grill for 45 minutes. Turn and continue to cook until the turkey skin is nicely browned and the internal temperature in a leg reaches 170 to 175°F (77 to 79°C), about 45 minutes. (Turkey legs have a lot of connective tissue and they seem to turn out better when cooked to a slightly higher temperature.)

6. Remove the legs from the grill and serve warm or cold.

Smoked Thanksgiving Turkey

Servings: 6 - 8
Cooking Time: 300 Minutes

Ingredients:
- 1 Turkey Brining Kits
- 12 – 14 Lbs Turkey
- 1 Gallon Water, Cold
- 4 Cups + 1 Gallon Water, Warm

Directions:

1. Start by defrosting the turkey overnight in the refrigerator.

2. Once turkey has been defrosted begin to make the brine by adding 4 cups of water and the brine mixture to a large stockpot.

3. Bring the mixture to a boil and add 1 gallon of cold water.

4. Place the turkey in the brine bag and pour the brine mixture over the turkey and refrigerate 1 hour per pound.

5. Once turkey has been brined rinse the turkey with cold water and set on a pan.

6. Using the seasoning in the brine box, season the turkey. Once turkey has been seasoned, supply your smoker with wood pellets and follow the start-up procedure. Preheat the grill, with the lid closed, to 275° F.

7. Place your turkey in the smoker and place the temperature probe in the deepest part of the breast. Cook at 275 until the breast and thigh meat internal temperature has reached 165°F to 170°F.

8. Remove the turkey from the smoker, let cool, and cut the turkey into your desired pieces. Enjoy!

Smoked Drumsticks

Servings: 2-4
Cooking Time: 25 Minutes

Ingredients:
- 1 pound chicken drumsticks
- 2 tablespoons olive oil
- 1 batch Sweet and Spicy Cinnamon Rub

Directions:

1. Supply your smoker with wood pellets and follow the start-up procedure. Preheat the grill, with the lid closed, to 350°F.

2. Coat the drumsticks all over with olive oil and season with the rub. Using your hands, work the rub into the meat.

3. Place the drumsticks directly on the grill grate and smoke until their internal temperature reaches 170°F. Remove the drumsticks from the grill and serve immediately.

Baked Garlic Parmesan Wings

Servings: 4
Cooking Time: 40 Minutes

Ingredients:
- 3 1/2 Tablespoon Chicken Rub
- 5 Pound chicken wings
- 1 Cup butter
- 10 Clove garlic, minced
- 1/2 Cup unsalted butter
- 10 Clove garlic, finely diced

- 1 Cup shredded Parmesan cheese
- 3 Tablespoon chopped parsley

Directions:

1. Supply your smoker with wood pellets and follow the start-up procedure. Preheat the grill, with the lid closed, to 450° F.

2. In a large bowl, toss the wings with the Traeger Chicken Rub.

3. Place wings directly on the grill grate and cook for 20 minutes. Flip wings and cook for an additional 20 minutes. Grill: 450 °F

4. Check the internal temperature of the wings, finished desired temperature is 165°F to 180°F. Grill: 450 °F Probe: 165 °F

5. To make the Garlic Sauce: While the chicken is cooking, combine butter, garlic and remaining rub in a medium sized saucepan and cook over medium heat on a stove top. Cook sauce for 8 to 10 minutes, stirring occasionally.

6. When wings are finished cooking, remove from grill and place in a large bowl. Toss wings with the garlic sauce, Parmesan cheese and parsley. Enjoy!

Grilled Hand Pulled Chicken

Servings: 4
Cooking Time: 90 Minutes

Ingredients:

- 2 Tablespoons Apple Cider Vinegar
- 1 Clove Garlic, Minced
- Juice Of Half Of A Lemon
- 1 Cup Mayo
- 1 Tablespoon Olive Oil
- ½ Teaspoon Paprika, Powder
- 2 Tablespoons Sugar
- 1, 3-4 Pound Chicken, Giblets Removed And Patted Dry

- 4 Tablespoons Champion Chicken Seasoning

Directions:

1. Supply your smoker with wood pellets and follow the start-up procedure. Preheat the grill, with the lid open, to 350° F.

2. In a large bowl, mix all the ingredients for the sauce together. Divide the sauce between two bowls and set aside.

3. On a clean, flat surface, lay your chicken breast side down. Using the kitchen shears, remove the spine and discard. Open the chicken up and flip the chicken over so that it lays breast side up. Press the breastbone down with the heel of your hand to flatten the chicken.

4. Generously rub the chicken with the olive oil and Champion Chicken. Place on the grill, skin-side up, on the grates. Grill for 1 ½ hours, basting with half the reserved sauce every 20 minutes, until the internal temperature reaches 175°F. Remove the chicken from the grill and cover loosely for 10 minutes.

5. Shred the chicken with forks and discard the skin and bones. Serve the chicken with the remaining white BBQ sauce.

Bbq Spatchcocked Chicken

Servings: 2
Cooking Time: 45 Minutes

Ingredients:

- 1 whole chicken
- 1/4 Cup Chicken Rub
- olive oil
- 1/2 Cup Sweet & Heat BBQ Sauce

Directions:

1. Supply your smoker with wood pellets and follow the start-up procedure. Preheat the grill, with the lid closed, to 375° F.

2. With a large knife or shears, cut the bird open along the backbone on both sides, through the ribs, and remove the backbone.

3. Brush chicken with olive oil and season both sides with Traeger Chicken rub.

4. Place the poultry on the Traeger, breast side up and cook for 35 to 40 minutes or until a thermometer inserted into the breast registers 160°F. Grill: 375 °F Probe: 160 °F

5. Remove from the grill and let rest 5 minutes before slicing. Enjoy!

Lollipop Drumsticks

Servings: 4-6

Cooking Time: 75 Minutes

Ingredients:

- 1 Cup Barbecue Sauce
- 10 Tablespoons Butter, Salted
- 12 Chicken Drumsticks
- 1 Cup Hot Sauce
- Champion Chicken Seasoning
- Blue Cheese Or Ranch Dressing

Directions:

1. Supply your smoker with wood pellets and follow the start-up procedure. Preheat the grill, with the lid open, to 300° F.

2. Rinse chicken and pat dry with a paper towel.

3. Chop the very top of the drumstick on the larger, meaty side so the lollipops sit flatly. On the small end of the drumstick, about an inch above the knuckle, use a sharp knife or kitchen shears to cut the skin and tendons all the way down to the bone and pull the skin and cartilage off the knuckle.

4. Remove the tiny, sharp bone that sits right against the exposed chicken leg. Then, push all the meat and skin down to form the lollipop ball.

Use your knife or shears to remove any excess tendons.

5. Season each lollipop generously with Champion Chicken seasoning and place in the aluminum pan with the flat side done and bones standing straight up. Then, cut 10 tablespoons of butter into cubes of 1 tablespoon each and place evenly throughout the rows of lollipops.

6. Cook lollipop drumsticks on your at 300°F for 1 hour; checking back every 20 minutes to baste the meat with the melted butter on the bottom of the pan.

7. For the Sauce: add your favorite bbq sauce into one aluminum loaf pan. Then, add 1 cup of hot sauce and 10 tablespoons of butter into the other aluminum loaf pan. Place them on the grill 5 minutes before your chicken is done. Stir well once it's warm and the butter has melted.

8. After 1 hour, use a thermometer to check the internal temperature of the lollipops. They will be ready to glaze when the temperature reaches 165°F.

9. Once ready, dip 6 lollipops in the bbq sauce and 6 in the buffalo sauce making sure to hold the leg and cover the meat entirely. Then, place the lollipops on the wing rack and put back on the grill for 15 more minutes or until the sauce is set.

Smoked Beer Garlic Chicken

Servings: 4

Cooking Time: 120 Minutes

Ingredients:

- 1 whole chicken
- 2 tbsp olive oil
- 1 tbsp salt
- 2 tsp thyme
- 2 tsp dill

- 2 tsp garlic powder
- 1 can beer

Directions:

1. Spray or rub olive oil on the outside of the chicken. In a bowl, mix all other ingredients together (except beer).

2. Rub this mixture on the outside of your chicken.

3. Fill the chicken stand with beer(takes about 3/4 of your can of beer).

4. Place chicken on top of the chicken stand. Supply your smoker with wood pellets and follow the start-up procedure. Preheat the grill, with the lid closed, to 350° F. place chicken in the center making sure it is flat and won't tip over(you can lean the chicken against the upper rack).

5. Allow the chicken to cook for 2 hours or until the internal temperature of the chicken reaches at least 165 °F.

6. Remove from the grill and the stand and let rest 5-10 minutes before carving. Serve. Enjoy!

Bbq Chicken Drumsticks

Servings: 4
Cooking Time: 120 Minutes

Ingredients:

- 8 chicken drumsticks
- 2 Tablespoon Chicken Rub
- 1/2 Cup 'Que BBQ Sauce

Directions:

1. Season each drumstick and let rest for 20 minutes.

2. Supply your smoker with wood pellets and follow the start-up procedure. Preheat the grill, with the lid closed, to 275° F.

3. Hang the drumsticks on the leg hanger (alternatively, place directly on the grill grate flipping halfway through) and cook for 1 hour. Grill: 275 °F

4. Remove the drumsticks from the hanger (or grate) and place in a pan. Grill: 275 °F Probe: 190 °F

5. Cover with foil and cook for 45 more minutes or until meat reaches an internal temperature of 190 degrees F. Grill: 275 °F Probe: 190 °F

6. Remove the foil and sauce all drumsticks in the pan.

7. Cook for an additional 15 minutes so sauce can set. Grill: 275 °F

8. Remove from Traeger and let rest for 15 minutes before serving. Enjoy!

Savory Smoked Turkey Legs

Servings: 4
Cooking Time: 150 Minutes

Ingredients:

- 1 Cup Chicken Stock
- 2 Tbsp Blackened Sriracha Rub
- 4 Turkey Legs (Drumsticks)

Directions:

1. Fire up your pellet grill on SMOKE mode. With the lid open, let it run for 10 minutes.

2. Supply your smoker with wood pellets and follow the start-up procedure. Preheat the grill, with the lid closed, to 225° F. If using a gas or charcoal grill, set it up for low, indirect heat.

3. Combine turkey stock with 2 teaspoons of Blackened Sriracha Rub.

4. Place turkey legs on a sheet tray, then inject each with seasoned stock. Season the outside of the legs with remaining Blackened Sriracha.

5. Place turkey legs directly on the grate of the smoking cabinet, and cook for 1 ½ hours.

6. Increase temperature to 325°F, then transfer turkey legs to the bottom grill and cook for another 45 to 60 minutes, until the internal temperature reaches 170°F.

7. Remove turkey from the grill, allow to rest for 10 minutes, then serve warm.

Whole Roasted Chicken

Servings: 4

Cooking Time: 60 Minutes

Ingredients:

- 1 Whole fresh young chicken
- 1 Bottle Chicken Rub
- water
- 1/2 Tablespoon kosher salt
- 1 Tablespoon chopped sage
- 1 Tablespoon chopped thyme
- 1/2 Cup butter, softened
- 1/2 Tablespoon coarse ground black pepper

Directions:

1. Remove whole chicken from packaging and wipe dry with a paper towel.

2. Mix water and chicken rub to create a brine. Place the chicken and brine in a container that's large enough to submerge the entire chicken.

3. Set in fridge for 4-12 hours.

4. Supply your smoker with wood pellets and follow the start-up procedure. Preheat the grill, with the lid closed, to 375° F.

5. Take chicken out of brine, do not rinse.

6. Mix together thyme, sage, salt, pepper and butter. Smear the outside of the chicken with the butter mixture. Put any of the remaining butter in the cavity of the chicken.

7. Place chicken directly on the grill grate. Cook chicken until it reaches an internal temperature of 165 degrees F (about 60 mins) with an instant-read thermometer between the leg and thigh joint. Grill: 375 ˚F Probe: 165 ˚F

8. Also check the internal temperature of the breast to ensure it registers at least 165 degrees F. Once chicken is done, let it rest for 15-20 minutes. Enjoy!

COCKTAILS RECIPES

Garden Gimlet Cocktail

Servings: 2
Cooking Time: 45 Minutes

Ingredients:

- 2 Cup honey
- 4 lemons, zested
- 4 Sprig rosemary, plus more for garnish
- 1/2 Cup water
- 4 Slices cucumber
- 1 1/2 Ounce lime juice
- 3 Ounce vodka

Directions:

1. Supply your smoker with wood pellets and follow the start-up procedure. Preheat the grill, with the lid closed, to 180° F.

2. To make smoked lemon and rosemary honey syrup, thin 1 cup honey by adding 1/4 cup water to a shallow pan. Add lemon zest and 2 sprigs rosemary.

3. Place the pan directly on the grill grate and smoke 45 minutes to an hour. Remove from heat, strain and cool. Grill: 180 °F

4. In a cocktail shaker, muddle the cucumbers and 1oz of the smoked lemon and rosemary honey syrup.

5. After muddling, add lime juice, vodka, and ice. Shake and double strain into a coup glass.

6. Garnish with a sprig of rosemary. Enjoy!

Smoked Irish Coffee

Servings: 2
Cooking Time: 15 Minutes

Ingredients:

- 10 Ounce hot coffee
- 1/2 Cup heavy cream
- 1 Tablespoon sugar
- 2 Ounce Irish whiskey
- freshly grated nutmeg, for garnish (optional)

Directions:

1. Supply your smoker with wood pellets and follow the start-up procedure. Preheat the grill, with the lid closed, to 180° F.

2. Place the coffee and cream in separate shallow baking dishes and place both directly on the grill grate. Smoke for 10 to 15 minutes until the liquids pick up a slight smoke flavor. Grill: 180 °F

3. Remove from the grill and cool the cream. When the cream is cool, add sugar and whip in a stand mixer or by hand to soft peaks.

4. Pour the hot coffee into two mugs then add 2 ounces of whiskey to each.

5. Top with smoked whipped cream and finish with freshly grated nutmeg, if desired. Enjoy!

Smoked Raspberry Bubbler Cocktail

Servings: 2
Cooking Time: 45 Minutes

Ingredients:

- 2 Cup fresh raspberries
- Smoked Simple Syrup
- 8 Ounce sparkling wine

Directions:

1. Supply your smoker with wood pellets and follow the start-up procedure. Preheat the grill, with the lid closed, to 180° F.

2. Smoked Raspberry Syrup: Place 1 cup fresh raspberries on a grill mat and smoke for 30 minutes. Grill: 180 °F

3. After the raspberries have been smoked, set a few aside for garnish. Place the remainder into a shallow sheet pan with Traeger Smoked Simple Syrup. Place back on the grill grate and let smoke for 45 minutes. Remove from heat and allow to cool. Strain and refrigerate until ready to use. Grill: 180 °F

4. Place 1 ounce of the smoked raspberry syrup in the bottom of a champagne flute and top off with sparkling white wine or champagne.

5. Garnish with smoked raspberries. Enjoy!

Dublin Delight Cocktail

Servings: 2

Cooking Time: 20 Minutes

Ingredients:

- 2 orange, sliced
- 3 Fluid Ounce Teeling Whiskey
- 1 1/2 Fluid Ounce Smoked Simple Syrup
- 6 Dash aromatic bitters
- 6 Fluid Ounce Guinness beer
- 2 Amarena cherry, for garnish

Directions:

1. Supply your smoker with wood pellets and follow the start-up procedure. Preheat the grill, with the lid closed, to 450° F.

2. Place orange slices directly on the grill grate and cook 20 to 25 minutes. Remove from grill and let cool. Grill: 450 °F

3. In a mixing glass, add whiskey, Traeger Smoked Simple Syrup and bitters. Add ice and shake. Pour over a beer glass filled with ice and top off with cold Guinness.

4. Garnish with a grilled orange slice and Amarena cherry. Enjoy!

Smoked Apple Cider

Servings: 2

Cooking Time: 30 Minutes

Ingredients:

- 32 Ounce apple cider
- 2 cinnamon sticks
- 4 whole cloves
- 3 star anise
- 2 Pieces orange peel
- 2 Pieces lemon peel

Directions:

1. Supply your smoker with wood pellets and follow the start-up procedure. Preheat the grill, with the lid closed, to 225° F.

2. Combine the cider, cinnamon stick, star anise, clove, lemon and orange peel in a shallow baking dish.

3. Place directly on the grill grate and smoke for 30 minutes. Remove from grill, strain and transfer to four mugs. Grill: 225 °F

4. Finish with a slice of apple and a cinnamon stick to serve. Enjoy!

Traeger Boulevardier Cocktail

Servings: 2

Cooking Time: 60 Minutes

Ingredients:

- 4 oranges
- 1/2 Cup honey
- 1500 mL rye whiskey
- 1 1/2 Ounce Campari
- 1 1/2 Ounce sweet vermouth
- 2 Tablespoon granulated sugar
- 3 Ounce grilled orange infused rye

Directions:

1. Supply your smoker with wood pellets and follow the start-up procedure. Preheat the grill, with the lid closed, to 350° F.

2. Slice 2 oranges in half and coat cut side with honey. Peel remaining orange and place peels on the grill. Cook 20 to 25 minutes. Grill: 350 °F

3. Remove from grill and let cool. Place orange halves cut side down directly on the grill grate and cook 20 to 30 minutes or until dark grill marks appear. Remove orange halves and allow to cool. Grill: 350 °F

4. Place orange halves into a bottle of rye whiskey and let steep for 10 to 12 hours. The longer they steep, the sweeter and more pronounced the orange flavor will be.

5. Add all ingredients into a mixing glass and stir until diluted. Strain into a fresh coupe glass and serve neat.

6. Garnish with grilled orange peel. Enjoy!

Smoked Salted Caramel White Russian

Servings: 4
Cooking Time: 20 Minutes

Ingredients:

- 16 Ounce half-and-half
- salted caramel sauce
- 6 Ounce vodka
- 6 Ounce Kahlúa

Directions:

1. Supply your smoker with wood pellets and follow the start-up procedure. Preheat the grill, with the lid closed, to 180° F.

2. Pour the half-and-half in a shallow baking dish and place directly on the grill grate. In another shallow baking dish, pour 2 to 3 cups of water and place on the grill next to the half-and-half.

3. Smoke both the half-and-half and water for 20 minutes. Remove from the grill and let cool. Grill: 180 °F

4. Place the half-and-half in the fridge until ready to use. Pour the smoked water into ice cube trays and transfer to the freezer until completely frozen.

5. Separate the smoked ice cubes into four glasses. Drizzle the salted caramel sauce around the inside of the glass.

6. Pour 1-1/2 ounce vodka and 1-1/2 ounce Kahlúa into each of the glasses and top with the smoked half-and-half. Enjoy!

Fig Slider Cocktail

Servings: 2
Cooking Time: 15 Minutes

Ingredients:

- 2 peach, halved
- 4 oranges
- honey
- sugar
- 2 Teaspoon orange fig spread
- 1 Ounce fresh lemon juice
- 4 Ounce bourbon
- 3 Ounce honey glazed grilled orange juice

Directions:

1. Supply your smoker with wood pellets and follow the start-up procedure. Preheat the grill, with the lid closed, to 325° F.

2. Pit the peach and cut in half. Cut one of the oranges in half. Glaze the peach and orange cut sides with honey and set directly on the grill grate until the honey caramelizes and fruit has grill marks. Grill: 325 °F

3. Cut the second orange into wheels and coat with granulated sugar on both sides. Place directly on the grill grate and cook 15 minutes each side or until grill marks form. Grill: 325 ˚F

4. In a mixing tin, add grilled peaches, bourbon, orange fig spread, fresh lemon juice and honey glazed orange juice.

5. Shake vigorously to blend the juices and fig spread. Strain over clean ice. Garnish with grilled orange wheel. Enjoy!

Zombie Cocktail Recipe

Servings: 2
Cooking Time: 45 Minutes

Ingredients:

- fresh squeezed orange juice
- pineapple juice
- 2 Ounce light rum
- 2 Ounce dark rum
- 2 Ounce lime juice
- 1 Ounce Smoked Simple Syrup
- 6 Ounce smoked orange and pineapple juice
- 2 grilled orange peel, for garnish
- 2 grilled pineapple chunks, for garnish

Directions:

1. Supply your smoker with wood pellets and follow the start-up procedure. Preheat the grill, with the lid closed, to 180° F.

2. Smoked Orange and Pineapple Juice: Pour equal parts fresh squeezed orange juice and pineapple juice into a shallow sheet pan and smoke for 45 minutes. Remove and let cool. Measure out 3 ounces of juice and reserve any remaining juice in the refrigerator for future use. Grill: 180 ˚F

3. Add dark and light rums, 3 ounces smoked orange and pineapple juice, lime juice and Traeger Smoked Simple Syrup to a mixing glass.

4. Add ice, shake and strain over clean ice into a Tiki glass.

5. Garnish with a grilled orange peel and grilled pineapple. Enjoy!

Smoked Texas Ranch Water

Servings: 4
Cooking Time: 60 Minutes

Ingredients:

- 3 Whole limes
- 1 Tablespoon Blackened Saskatchewan Rub
- 12 Ounce blanco tequila
- 24 Ounce Topo Chico or other sparkling mineral water
- 8 Slices jalapeño, optional

Directions:

1. Supply your smoker with wood pellets and follow the start-up procedure. Preheat the grill, with the lid closed, to 225° F.

2. Cut two of the limes in half and sprinkle with Traeger Blackened Saskatchewan Rub. Place the four lime halves on the edge of the grill grate and smoke for 1 hour. Remove from grill and set aside to cool. Grill: 225 ˚F

3. Pour some of the rub onto a small plate. Cut the third lime into 1/4 wedges and use the lime to rub the rim of 4 cocktail glasses, turn the glasses upside down, and into the rub to salt the rim.

4. Place several ice cubes into your rimmed glasses and pour 3 ounces tequila, 6 ounces Topo Chico, squeeze the juice of one smoked lime (discard after squeezing), and add one fresh lime wedge to each. If using the jalapeño, add one or two slices to each glass (muddle if desired).

5. Stir to combine and enjoy!

Traeger Gin & Tonic

Servings: 2

Cooking Time: 45 Minutes

Ingredients:

- 1/2 Cup berries
- 2 orange, sliced
- 4 Tablespoon granulated sugar
- 3 Ounce gin
- 1 Cup tonic water
- 2 Sprig fresh mint, for garnish

Directions:

1. Supply your smoker with wood pellets and follow the start-up procedure. Preheat the grill, with the lid closed, to 180° F.

2. For the Smoked Berries: Spread mixed fresh berries on a sheet pan and place directly on the grill grate. Smoke for 30 minutes then remove from grill. Grill: 180 °F

3. For the Orange Slices: Increase the grill temperature to 450°F and preheat, lid closed for 15 minutes. Grill: 450 °F

4. Toss the orange slices with granulated sugar and place directly on grill grate. Cook for about 5 minutes, turning once or until the slices have developed grill marks. Grill: 450 °F

5. Pour gin into a glass, add ice and berries, then top with tonic water. Garnish with a fresh mint sprig and grilled orange wheel. Enjoy!

Smoked Sangria

Servings: 6

Cooking Time: 45 Minutes

Ingredients:

- 1 (750 ml) medium-bodied red wine
- 1/4 Cup Grand Marnier
- 1/4 Cup Smoked Simple Syrup
- 1 Cup fresh cranberries
- 1 Whole apple, sliced
- 2 Whole limes, sliced
- 4 cinnamon stick
- soda water

Directions:

1. Supply your smoker with wood pellets and follow the start-up procedure. Preheat the grill, with the lid closed, to 180° F.

2. In a shallow dish, combine red wine, Grand Marnier, Traeger Smoked Simple Syrup and cranberries, and place directly on the grill grate.

3. Smoke for 30 to 45 minutes or until the liquid picks up desired amount of smoke. Remove from grill and place in the fridge to cool. Grill: 180 °F

4. When the mixture has cooled, place in a large pitcher. Add sliced apples, limes, cinnamon sticks and ice to pitcher.

5. Top with soda water, if desired. Enjoy!

Grilled Hawaiian Sour

Servings: 2

Cooking Time: 15 Minutes

Ingredients:

- 2 Whole pineapple, trimmed and sliced
- 1/2 Cup palm sugar
- 3 Ounce bourbon
- 2 Ounce grilled pineapple juice
- 2 Ounce Smoked Simple Syrup
- 10 Ounce lemon juice
- 2 grilled pineapple chunk, for garnish
- 2 pineapple leaf, for garnish

Directions:

1. Supply your smoker with wood pellets and follow the start-up procedure. Preheat the grill, with the lid closed, to 350° F.

2. For the Grilled Pineapple Juice: Dust pineapple slices with palm sugar. Place directly on the grill grate and cook for 8 minutes per side. Grill: 350 °F

3. Remove from grill and let cool. Reserve a few pieces for garnish. Run remaining pineapple pieces through centrifugal juicer to extract juice.

4. To Make the Drink: Add bourbon, grilled pineapple juice, simple syrup and lemon juice to a cocktail strainer with ice. Shake vigorously. Double strain into a chilled coupe glass. Garnish with grilled pineapple chunk and pineapple leaf. Enjoy!

Smoky Mountain Bramble Cocktail

Servings: 2

Cooking Time: 15 Minutes

Ingredients:

- 16 Ounce blackberries
- 2 Cup sugar
- 10 smoked blackberries
- 3 Ounce vodka
- 1 1/2 Ounce Alpine Distilling Preserve Liqueur
- 1 1/2 Ounce lemon juice
- 1 Ounce smoked blackberry syrup

Directions:

1. Supply your smoker with wood pellets and follow the start-up procedure. Preheat the grill, with the lid closed, to 180° F.

2. To make Smoked Blackberry Simple Syrup: Place blackberries on a grill mat and smoke for 15 to 20 minutes. Grill: 180 °F

3. Combine 1 cup water and sugar in a small sauce pan and warm over medium heat until sugar dissolves. Remove from heat and place 2/3 of blackberries in the simple syrup and macerate.

4. Strain through a fine mesh strainer and store for up to 14 days.

5. To make the cocktail: Muddle 4 to 5 smoked blackberries in a cocktail shaker. Add vodka, Preserve Liqueur, lemon and smoked blackberry syrup. Add ice and shake vigorously. Double strain into an old fashioned glass.

6. Garnish with a smoked blackberry and lemon twist. Enjoy!

In Traeger Fashion Cocktail

Servings: 2

Cooking Time: 20 Minutes

Ingredients:

- 2 Whole orange peel
- 2 Whole lemon peel
- 3 Ounce bourbon
- 1 Ounce Smoked Simple Syrup
- 6 Dash Bitters Lab Charred Cedar & Currant Bitters

Directions:

1. Supply your smoker with wood pellets and follow the start-up procedure. Preheat the grill, with the lid closed, to 350° F.

2. Place the lemon and orange peel directly on the grill grate and cook 20 to 25 minutes or until lightly browned. Grill: 350 °F

3. Add bourbon, Traeger Smoked Simple Syrup and bitters to a mixing glass and stir over ice. Stir until glass is chilled and contents are well diluted.

4. Strain into a new glass over fresh ice and garnish with grilled lemon and orange peel. Enjoy!

Smoky Scotch & Ginger Cocktail

Servings: 2
Cooking Time: 60 Minutes

Ingredients:

- 1 Ounce ginger syrup
- 1/2 Ounce brandied cherry juice
- 1/2 Ounce agave nectar
- 4 Ounce scotch
- 1 1/2 Ounce lemon juice
- 2 Slices grilled lemon, for garnish
- 2 cherry, for garnish

Directions:

1. Supply your smoker with wood pellets and follow the start-up procedure. Preheat the grill, with the lid closed, to 180° F.

2. For the smoked ginger cherry syrup: Place ginger syrup, cherry juice and agave nectar in a shallow dish and place the dish directly on the grill grate.

3. Smoke for 60 minutes, or until the mixture has picked up the smoke flavor. Remove from grill and allow to cool for 30 minutes. Grill: 180 °F

4. Place smoked ginger cherry syrup, scotch and lemon juice into a shaker tin and shake with ice. Strain into a glass over fresh ice and garnish with a grilled lemon wheel and cherry. Enjoy!

Smoked Berry Cocktail

Servings: 2
Cooking Time: 15 Minutes

Ingredients:

- 1/2 Cup strawberries, stemmed
- 1/2 Cup blackberries
- 1/2 Cup blueberries
- 8 Ounce bourbon or iced tea
- 2 Ounce lime juice
- 3 Ounce simple syrup
- soda water
- fresh mint, for garnish

Directions:

1. Supply your smoker with wood pellets and follow the start-up procedure. Preheat the grill, with the lid closed, to 180° F.

2. Wash berries well, spread them on a clean cookie sheet and place on the grill. Smoke berries for 15 minutes. Grill: 180 °F

3. Remove berries from grill and transfer to a blender. Puree berries until smooth then pass through a fine mesh strainer to remove seeds.

4. To create a layered cocktail, pour 2 ounces of berry puree in the bottom of a glass. Next, pour 2 ounces of bourbon or iced tea over the back of a spoon into the glass, then 1/2 ounce lime juice and 1/2 ounce simple syrup, top with soda water and ice. Finish with mint or extra berries for garnish.

5. Repeat the same process for 3 more servings. Enjoy!

Grilled Rabbit Tail Cocktail

Servings: 2
Cooking Time: 25 Minutes

Ingredients:

- 1 1/2 Ounce lemon juice
- 4 Ounce Apple Brandy
- 1 Ounce orange juice
- 1 Ounce Smoked Simple Syrup

Directions:

1. Supply your smoker with wood pellets and follow the start-up procedure. Preheat the grill, with the lid closed, to 350° F.

2. Place lemon halves directly on the grill grate and cook for 20-25 minutes or until grill marks appear. Remove from grill and let cool. Once cool enough to handle, juice the lemons then chill and reserve the juice. Grill: 350 ˚F

3. Using the proportions listed above and considering the size and consumption rate of your tailgate crew or party, mix all the above ingredients in a large thermos and top with a bit of ice.

4. Using 6-8 oz glasses or cups, guests can serve themselves from the thermos and garnish each drink with a grilled apple slice. Enjoy!

Smoked Plum And Thyme Fizz Cocktail

Servings: 2

Cooking Time: 60 Minutes

Ingredients:

- 6 fresh plums
- 4 Fluid Ounce vodka
- 1 1/2 Fluid Ounce fresh lemon juice
- 2 Ounce smoked plum and thyme simple syrup
- 4 Fluid Ounce club soda
- 2 Slices smoked plum, for garnish
- 2 Sprig fresh thyme, for garnish
- 8 Sprig thyme
- 2 Cup Smoked Simple Syrup

Directions:

1. Supply your smoker with wood pellets and follow the start-up procedure. Preheat the grill, with the lid closed, to 180° F.

2. Cut plums in half and remove the pit. Place the plum halves directly on the grill grate and smoke for 25 minutes. Grill: 180 ˚F

3. For the Plum and Thyme Simple Syrup: After 25 minutes, remove plums from the grill and cut into quarters. Add plums and thyme sprigs to 1 cup of Traeger Smoked Simple Syrup. Smoke the mixture for 45 minutes. Remove from grill, strain and let cool. Grill: 180 ˚F

4. Add vodka, fresh lemon juice and smoked plum and thyme simple syrup to a mixing glass.

5. Add ice and shake. Strain over clean ice, top off with club soda and garnish with a piece of thyme and slice of smoked plum. Enjoy!

Smoked Mulled Wine

Servings: 10

Cooking Time: 60 Minutes

Ingredients:

- 2 Bottle red wine
- 1/2 Cup whiskey
- 1/2 Cup white rum
- 1/2 Cup honey
- 1 cinnamon stick
- 2 pods star anise
- 4 whole cloves
- 1 (3 in) orange peel

Directions:

1. Supply your smoker with wood pellets and follow the start-up procedure. Preheat the grill, with the lid closed, to 180° F.

2. In a shallow baking dish, combine wine, whiskey, rum, honey, cinnamon stick, star anise, cloves and orange peel. Stir well until combined.

3. Place the dish directly on the grill grate and smoke for one hour until the mixture is warm. Grill: 180 ˚F

4. Remove from grill and ladle into mugs leaving the mulling spices behind. Garnish with fresh cinnamon sticks, anise, orange zest or a combination. Enjoy!

Traeger Smoked Daiquiri

Servings: 2

Cooking Time: 25 Minutes

Ingredients:

- 2 limes, sliced
- 2 Tablespoon granulated sugar
- 3 Ounce Rum
- 1 Ounce Smoked Simple Syrup
- 1 1/2 Ounce lime juice

Directions:

1. Supply your smoker with wood pellets and follow the start-up procedure. Preheat the grill, with the lid closed, to 350° F.

2. Toss the lime slices with granulated sugar and place directly on the grill grate. Cook 20-25 minutes or until grill marks form. Remove from grill and cool. Grill: 350 ˚F

3. In a mixing glass add rum, Traeger Simple Syrup, and fresh lime juice. Add ice to the mixing glass and shake. Strain contents into a chilled glass.

4. Garnish with a grilled lime wheel. Enjoy!

Grilled Frozen Strawberry Lemonade

Servings: 4

Cooking Time: 15 Minutes

Ingredients:

- 1 Pound fresh strawberries
- 1/2 Cup turbinado sugar
- 8 lemon, halved
- 1/4 Cup Cointreau
- 1/4 Cup simple syrup
- 2 Cup ice
- 1 Cup Titos Vodka

Directions:

1. Supply your smoker with wood pellets and follow the start-up procedure. Preheat the grill, with the lid closed, to High heat.

2. Dip the lemon halves in turbinado sugar and place directly on the grill grate. Toss the strawberries with remaining sugar and place next to the lemons.

3. Cook until grill marks develop on both, about 15 min for lemons and 10 min for strawberries.

4. Remove from heat and let cool.

5. Juice grilled lemons straining out any seeds or pulp. Pour into a blender pitcher.

6. Remove stems from grilled strawberries and place in blender pitcher with lemon juice. Add simple syrup, vodka, cointreau, and 2 cups of ice.

7. Puree until smooth and transfer to 4-6 glasses. Garnish with grilled strawberries and grilled lemon slices if desired. Enjoy!

Grilled Peach Sour Cocktail

Servings: 2

Cooking Time: 15 Minutes

Ingredients:

- 2 peach, sliced
- 2 Tablespoon sugar

- 1 1/2 Ounce Smoked Simple Syrup
- 4 Ounce bourbon
- 6 Dash Bitters Lab Apricot Vanilla Bitters
- 2 Sprig fresh thyme, for garnish

Directions:

1. Supply your smoker with wood pellets and follow the start-up procedure. Preheat the grill, with the lid closed, to 325° F.

2. Toss peach slices with granulated sugar and place directly on grill grate. Cook for 20 minutes or until grill marks form. Remove from grill and let cool. Grill: 325 °F

3. Place peaches and Traeger Smoked Simple Syrup into tin and muddle. Peaches should form about an ounce of juice during the muddling. Once completed, add remaining ingredients and shake.

4. Pour contents into glass over fresh ice and garnish with fresh thyme. Enjoy!